Additional

The 101 Biggest Estate Planning Mistakes

"Estate mediators beware. This little book could put you out of business."

—Robert B. Davidson, JAMS

"Herb Nass has once again written a book that is not only a valuable resource, but interesting and fun to read. If the book was called *102 Biggest Estate Planning Mistakes,* the 102nd mistake would be to not read this book. As Herb Nass points out, "He who fails to plan, plans to fail." I would recommend this book to all my clients."

—Jeffrey S. Gerson, Director, Wealth Management
Morgan Stanley Smith Barney, LLC

"Estate planning mistakes can and will have a profound impact on future generations. *The 101 Biggest Estate Planning Mistakes* is an entertaining view of serious personal business."

—Peter C. Valente, Partner, Trusts & Estates
Blank Rome LLP

"Who would believe that a book about estate planning could actually be fun to read? Attorney Herb Nass has organized 101 possible estate planning mistakes in a brilliant and lucid manner, and has made this a "must read" for anyone who is going to die, even if you are not planning to die anytime soon, and even if you are a lawyer. I loved it."

—Raoul Felder, Raoul Felder and Partners, P.C.

"Herb Nass shows that in estate planning, common mistakes can lead to uncommon—and costly—consequences. Here's a book that can help you avoid many of them."

—Martin Grant, Financial Advisor
Bernstein Global Wealth Management

"Herb Nass has a unique ability to convey important legal concepts in a straightforward, accessible style. *The 101 Biggest Estate Planning Mistakes* is no exception. Both professionals and laypeople will enjoy and benefit from this helpful book."

—Peter Culver, Senior Director
BNY Mellon Wealth Management

"Herb Nass' latest literary legal gem will point laypersons in the right direction and is an invaluable desk book and guide for every estate planner."

—William Schwartz, Esq., Cadwalader,
Wickersham & Taft LLP

The 101 Biggest Estate Planning Mistakes

Herbert E. Nass, Esq.

WILEY

John Wiley & Sons, Inc.

Published by John Wiley & Sons, Inc., Hoboken, New Jersey.
Published simultaneously in Canada.

For general information on our other products and services, or for technical support, please
contact our Customer Care Department within the United States at (800) 762-2974, outside
the United States at (317) 572-3993, or via fax (317) 572-4002.

Wiley also publishes its books in a variety of electronic formats. Some content that appears in
print may not be available in electronic books. For more information about Wiley products,
visit our web site at www.wiley.com.

Library of Congress Cataloging-in-Publication Data:

Nass, Herbert E.
    The 101 biggest estate planning mistakes / Herbert E Nass.
       p.   cm.
    Includes index.
    ISBN 978-0-470-37503-7 (pbk.)
    1. Estate planning–United States.   I. Title.   II. Title: One hundred one biggest estate
planning mistakes.
    KF750.N37 2009
    346.7305'2–dc22

10 9 8 7 6 5 4 3 2 1

Dedicated to:

*My wonderful wife Jodi, whose energy,
resourcefulness, and effervescence continue
to be great sources of inspiration
and support for me;*

and

*Our two impressive children, Stephanie and Teddy,
who are growing up so beautifully
and of whom we are very proud.*

*Thank you all for giving me the time
and "space" to write this book.*

*H.E.N.
May 31, 2009*

Contents

Contents

Contents

Contents

Contents

Contents

Contents

Contents

Contents

Preface

As an attorney practicing in the area of estate planning and trust and estate administration for more than 25 years at a big law firm (Paul, Weiss, Rifkind, Wharton & Garrison), at a medium-size law firm (Tenzer, Greenblatt, Fallon & Kaplan) and at a small law firm (Herbert E. Nass & Associates), I have seen and learned many things about the estate planning practice. I have witnessed, and often cleaned up, the problems that can arise when mistakes are made in the preparation of estate planning documents or in the administration of a trust or an estate. I have even made a few mistakes myself, but never the same mistake twice.

Over the course of my career, I have prepared and supervised the due and proper execution of thousands of Wills and handled hundreds of estates, both large and small. While handling those estates, I have represented numerous clients and met many characters. Most of them were quite nice and reputable, but there were a few shady ones as well.

In this book, I will share the 101 estate planning mistakes that I have seen—and helped my clients avoid—along the way.

The mistakes described in this book run the gamut from the mundane to the arcane, and the ramifications of these mistakes can be nearly meaningless or of great significance from a financial and/ or emotional point of view. In some ways, this book is intended to be a guide for what *not* to do in your estate planning.

* * *

In the course of my legal career, I have had the privilege of assisting many smart, important, and even famous people with their estate planning. Of course, all of our clients are important, but some of the famous ones have included one of the greatest artists of the 20th century, one of the greatest actresses, one of the greatest, if not the greatest, baseball player/manager of all time, and even a few famous rock-and-roll stars. It is certainly an honor for us to assist people who are leaders in their fields, and we always do our best to avoid making these or any other mistakes when representing our clients.

In examples of mistakes that are based on my own experiences involving our clients, we have changed the names to protect the innocent (or the stupid). However, many of the most interesting mistakes involve celebrities about whom we have all heard and read. For example, Queen Leona Helmsley, in my opinion, made four mistakes in her Will, including leaving too much money to her pet (#16), not compensating the executors of her Will (#33), disinheriting her grandchildren out of anger or vindictiveness (#68), and directing that her pet's remains be buried with her own (#84). As is more fully described in each of those sections, Leona made some big mistakes, but that may just be a function of the fact that she had a very big estate and a dog named Trouble(with a capital T).

But Leona Helmsley is not the only celebrity to make mistakes. We can have fun (and learn) by examining the nonsensical Will of Anna Nicole Smith (#40 and #45) and the Wills of many of my favorite musicians and performers, including Jim Morrison (#89), John Lennon (#41), Sonny Bono (#1), Ray Charles (#5), and Sammy Davis, Jr. (#9).

Many of the Beautiful People, including Jackie O. (#11), Andy Warhol (#14), Princess Diana (#86), and Doris Duke (#39) may have made some mistakes in their Wills or in the administration of their estates as well.

But even the "little people," whom Leona Helmsley was infamous for saying were the ones who paid taxes, also make mistakes, and the 101 Biggest are full of these too.

Mistakes come in all shapes and sizes, and for the purpose of this book, which is often a guide as to what *not* to do, the 101 mistakes that I discuss have been divided into the following 11 chapters, each with one central theme:

1. The Single Biggest Mistake Is Not Planning for the One Certainty in Life...Death
2. Mistakes Involving Tangible Personal Property
3. Mistakes Involving Real Estate
4. Mistakes Involving Executors and/or Trustees
5. Mistakes Involving Guardians, Minors, or Step-Children
6. Mistakes Involving Prior Marriages, Prenuptial Agreements, and Significant Others
7. Mistakes Involving Tax and Copyright Issues
8. Mistakes Involving Disgruntled Friends and Family
9. Mistakes Involving Funerals, Burials, or Cremation
10. One-of-a-Kind Mistakes by Celebrities and Icons
11. Rookie or Bonehead Mistakes

Although the book will flow best reading from start to finish, there is no reason not to start reading the chapter that is on your mind at the moment.

I hope and trust that all of my readers will benefit from my experience as a practicing attorney in these fields for many years and will avoid making any of these 101 mistakes.

Acknowledgments

So many people have been supportive of me and this endeavor, and I would like to thank all of you. In particular, the following people deserve special thanks for their inspiration and/or assistance:

Jane Dystel

Ann, Richard, and Bill Sarnoff

Matthew Rich

Jenifer Weis & John Monsky, Esq.

Jeffrey S. Gerson

Harlan M. Stone

Linda Bell Blue

Glen Meehan

Erin and Dr. Seth Neubardt

Paola and James H. Miller

Barbara and Tom Kornreich

Jill and Matthew Cantor, Esqs.

Nancy Friedman-Margolin

Michael Kaminsky, Esq.

Carol and Franklin Speyer

Betty and Fred Hayman

Renata, Martin, and Henry Zimet

Dr. Ruth Nass and Teddy Gross

Amanda and Seth Miller

Sandy Neubardt, Esq.

J. Edward Meyer, Esq.

William Schwartz, Esq.

Michael Bourret

Shelley and Donald Meltzer

Donald J. Trump

Josh Manheimer

Pam and Len Yablon

Kay Murray, Esq.

Bonnie Tiegel

Rick Joyce

Denice and Robert Hayman

Michael Grossman

Andrew Neubardt, Esq.

Marina and Steven Lowy

Sian Ballen Speiser

Fran Weinstein

Wendy and Lewis Rubin

Ivan Jenson

Victor Matthews

Abbe and Greg Large

Brian and Ed Herbst

Ron Herbst, Esq.

Adina Zion, Esq.

Linda and Brian Tell

Acknowledgments

Jennifer and Steve Warner

Linda and Mitchell Berger

Daryn & David Grossman, Esqs.

Tom Danziger, Esq.

Joan Rivers

Bill Zysblat

Steve Ludsin

Lucy Klingenstein & Brandon Sall, Esq.
Mark Kostabi

Hilary and Jeff Suchman

Linda and David Simon

Liz and Richard Kadin

William D. Zabel, Esq.

Dayna Langfan and Larry Heller

Amy and David Nachman, Esqs.

Peggy and Andrew Wallach

Oprah Winfrey

Douglas Martin

James Barron

Nancy J. Friedman

Everett Weinberger

John Erman
Richard Blair

David Jacoby, Esq.

David Washburn, Esq.

Steven Vlock, Esq.

Mark Risk, Esq.

Peter C. Valente, Esq,

Doug Schoen

Meg and Bob Ebin, Esqs.

Darlene Orlov

Arlene and Stephan Bassett

Rex Reed

Kenneth J. Stumpf

Rhoda Kadin

Robin Leach

Lia and Larry Shire, Esq.

Elaine Sargent

Ginny and Brian Ruder
Karen and Mark Hauser

Barbara and Herb Louis

Marcy and Paul Kadin

Nina and Pieter Taselaar

Claire and Larry Benenson

Burt and Leni Welte

Robert Steinberg, Esq.

Larry King

Bob Koo

Richard Johnson

Steven Giordano, Esq.

David Chen

Adam Coopersmith, CPA

Peter Culver
Kevin Rodman

Beverly Shackman, Esq.

Jan and Lloyd Constantine, Esqs.

Martin E. Fleisher, Esq.

Steven C. Bennett, Esq.

Alan Halperin, Esq.

Ralph Schlissberg, CPA

Silda and Eliot Spitzer, Esqs.

Claudia and Mario Covo

Acknowledgments

Brett Rosen

Joshua Mondschein

Steven H. Goodman

Francis Chimenti

Al Weil

Stefan L. Weill

Daniel J. Draddy

Jay Goldberg, CPA

Michael Warshauer, Esq

Steven J. Brandfield

Ted James

Marc Kazmac

Jon Olson, Esq.

Nancy and Brad Benjamin

Caroline and Jon Rosen

Sidney Kess, CPA, Esq.

Biff Liff

Elizabeth Pressman Neubardt

Ali and Joe Torre

David Finkelstein, Esq.

Nancy and Ken Dressler

Thomas J. Carstens

Peter Haines

David Singer, Esq.

Ellen and Robert Shasha

Christopher Guarino

Richard DiVenuto

Michael Gammarati

Martin Shenkman, Esq.

Cindy Calderon Rega

Rorie Sherman

Alan R. Finkelstein

Jeffrey S. Weiss

Mitchell Ostrove

James M. Luongo

Dana and Robert Blum

Alex Conti

Bob Jurgens, CPA

Henry E. Nass

Cosme Marley

Gail and Walter Harris

Elizabeth and Mallory Factor

Robert D. Gries

Robert Sonnenblick

Candy and Michael
Barasch, Esqs.

Gil Parker

Barry Carron

Adrian Benepe

Seth Slotkin, Esq.

Susan and Dan Shaffer

Michael Book

Rick Van Benschoten

Bob Davidson, Esq.

Rochelle and Mark Rosenberg

Gregory Meisel

Shawn Landau

Frank Augustine

Martin Grant

Lauren Barrett

Acknowledgments

Last, but cetainly not least, I must credit the important assistance of my Associate, Edward Romanello, and thank him for his tireless and dedicated work related to the production of the manuscript. I would also like to acknowledge my Senior Paralegal, Jane Sun Kim, for her written contributions to a few of the sections of the 101 included in this book.

1

The Single Biggest Mistake Is Not Planning for the One Certainty in Life . . . Death

There are many reasons that an estate plan is not properly effectuated.

The examples used in this first chapter are stories of lost souls, lost Wills, or Wills that were not properly executed or were far out of date. Sometimes, people could just care less about attending to their estate planning and what happens after they are gone. Many people may also rest on false premises, believing that the estate plan that was executed 10 or 20 years ago is still current and effective, as seen in the very out-of-date Wills of Robert F. Kennedy and Ted Ammon. Some might have the best intentions, but just don't get it done because they cannot sign a Will due to a physical disability. With proper legal advice, a Will can be duly executed, as shown by the blind Ray Charles and paralyzed Christopher Reeve. And sometimes a person may think that he has a Will, but a Judge in a court or several courts of law may disrespectfully disagree, as some of the hopeful named beneficiaries of Howard Hughes found out the hard way in the estate mess that he left behind.

Whatever the reason that an estate plan is not ultimately found to be valid or effective, the ramifications and problems that result can be quite serious, so be sure to avoid all of the mistakes outlined in this first chapter, which describes all the ways to make the single biggest mistake.

Mistake #1: **No Estate Planning Whatsoever**

Question: What do all of the following people have in common?

President Abraham Lincoln	Martin Luther King, Jr.
Rita Hayworth	Jayne Mansfield
Pablo Picasso	Jean-Michel Basquiat
Sonny Bono	Lenny Bruce
Chris Farley	Florence Joyner
Sal Mineo	Dylan Thomas
Peter Tosh	Bob Marley
Tupac Shakur	Keith Moon
George Gershwin	John Coltrane
John Denver	Peter Lorre
Howard Hughes	

Answer: They all died without a valid Last Will and Testament.

How do I know this? Because I have copies of the court files about their estates, indicating that each of them died *intestate*—that is, without a valid Last Will and Testament. Those files are all a matter of public record and can make for fascinating reading.

In addition to all the famous people mentioned above, most Americans die without a valid Will, which often leads to unnecessary expenses, complications, and dreaded taxes. If you don't have a Will, the laws of the state where you are domiciled at the time of your death determine who will get your property, when they will get your property, and who will be the person or public administrator to administer your estate and take care of any minor children.

Although my friend, the film director Spike Lee, once told me quite bluntly that he did not like the concept behind my first book, *Wills of the Rich & Famous*, and did not believe that his Will, nor anybody else's, should be a matter of public record, I respectfully disagree with Mr. Lee. For the ownership of property to be transferred in a manner that leaves a clear record of how the title to such property came to be in the name of the present owner, there also needs to be a way for a claimant or creditor of a decedent to be able to assert claims against the decedent's estate, so the name and address of the executor of the Will needs to be readily accessible.

Following are copies of the court papers related to the intestate estates of singer, entertainer, and U.S. Congressman Sonny Bono (Exhibit 1.1) and rapper Tupac Shakur (Exhibit 1.2), whose estates were administered in Los Angeles, California. The partial inventory of the tangible personal property in the estate of 25-year-old Tupac Shakur makes for some especially bling-bling reading.

And let us not forget reggae, whose most famous son was Bob Marley. His estate was subject to the jurisdiction of the Supreme Court of Judicature of Jamaica, and the court papers for his estate reveal that his largest asset, other than his musical talent, may have been a company called Tuff Gong Records Limited. (See Exhibit 1.3.)

The great American civil rights leader Dr. Martin Luther King was assassinated in 1968. He died without a Will, left a widow, Coretta Scott King, and four young children. His estate was subject to the jurisdiction of the Fulton County Court of Ordinary in Georgia, and the court papers reveal that his widow needed to post a $20,000 bond for her husband's estate.[1] That cost would have been avoided if Dr. King had seen a lawyer to prepare a Last Will and Testament, which usually expressly states that the executor need not post any bond.

Each of these people had his or her own reasons for not signing and leaving behind a Will. However, sometimes the Will existed but cannot be found. Sometimes, disgruntled relatives or friends

---

| HENRY N. JANNOL, ESQ. (Bar #86309)
HENRY N. JANNOL, A PROFESSIONAL
CORPORATION
1875 CENTURY PARK EAST #1400
LOS ANGELES, CA 90067
310-552-7500
ATTORNEY FOR (Name): MARY BONO | M. NEIL SOLARZ, ESQ. (Ear #78259)
WEINSTOCK, MANION, REISMAN,
SHORE & NEUMANN
1888 CENTURY PARK EAST #800
LOS ANGELES, CA 90067
310-553-8844 | FOR COURT USE ONLY

F I L E D
RIVERSIDE COUNTY

FEB 23 1998

ARTHUR A. SIMS, Clerk
By R. Gonzales
R. Gonzales Deputy |

SUPERIOR COURT OF CALIFORNIA, COUNTY OF RIVERSIDE
STREET ADDRESS: 46-200 Oasis Street
MAILING ADDRESS: 46-200 Oasis Street
CITY AND ZIP CODE: Indio, California 92201
BRANCH NAME: Indio Branch (Desert Judicial District)

ESTATE OF (Name): SALVATORE PHILLIP BONO

DECEDENT

| PETITION FOR | ☐ Probate of Will and for Letters Testamentary
☐ Probate of Will and for Letters of Administration
   with Will Annexed
☒ Letters of Administration
☐ Letters of Special Administration
☒ Authorization to Administer Under the Independent
   Administration of Estates Act ☐ with limited authority | CASE NUMBER
FP15865

HEARING DATE:
MAR 25 1998

DATE: 3P TIME: 8:45 AM |

1. Publication will be in (specify name of newspaper): THE DESERT SUN
   a. ☒ Publication requested.   b. ☐ Publication to be arranged.   **requests**
2. **Petitioner** (name of each): MARY BONO
   a. ☐ decedent's will and codicils, if any, be admitted to probate.
   b. ☒ (name): MARY BONO
      be appointed   (1) ☐ executor   (3) ☒ administrator
                     (2) ☐ administrator with will annexed (4) ☐ special administrator
      and Letters issue upon qualification.
   c. ☒ that   c. ☒ full   c. ☐ limited   authority be granted to administer under the independent
                                             Administration of Estates Act.
   d. (1) ☐ bond not be required for the reasons stated in item 3d.
      (2) ☒ $ 1,700,000 bond be fixed. If will be furnished by an admitted surety insurer or as otherwise provided
         by law (Specify reasons in Attachment 2 if the amount is different from the maximum required by
         Probate Code section 8482.)
      (3) ☐ $ in deposits in a blocked account be allowed. Receipts will be filed.
                                     (Specify institution and location):
3. a. Decedent died on (date): 1/5/98   at (place): Stateline, Nevada
      (1) ☒ a resident of the county named above.
      (2) ☐ a nonresident of California and left an estate in the county named above located at (specify
         location permitting publication in the newspaper named in item 1):
   b. Street address, city, and county of decedent's residence at time of death (specify):
      301 W. El Camino Way, Palm Springs, CA 92264, County of Riverside
   c. Character and estimated value of the property of the estate:
      (1) Personal property: $ 1,550,000.00
      (2) Annual gross income from
         (a) real property: $
         (b) Personal property: $ 150,000.00
                          Total: $ 1,700,000.00
      (3) Real property: $ 0   (If full authority under the Independent Administration of Estates
                                      Act is requested, state the fair market value of the real property
                                      less encumbrances.)
   d. (1) ☐ Will waives bond.   ☐ Special administrator is the named executor and the will waives bond.
      (2) ☐ All beneficiaries are adults and have waived bond, and the will does not require a bond. (Affix
         waiver as Attachment 3d(2).)
      (3) ☐ All heirs at law are adults and have waived bond. (Affix waiver as Attachment 3d(3).)
      (4) ☐ Sole personal representative is a corporate fiduciary or an exempt government agency.

| Form approved by the
Judicial Council of California
DE-111 (Rev. January 1, 1998) | PETITION FOR PROBATE | Probate Code. §§ 8002, 10450
CEB |

Exhibit 1.1 California court papers for the estate of Sonny Bono

Source: Sonny Bono, Intestate, Case Number FP 15865, Superior Court of California, County of Riverside, Indio, CA.

ESTATE OF (name)		CASE NUMBER
SALVATORE PHILLIP BONO	DECEDENT	ɪ ŀ ɪ⊃.⊲ᶜᵘ

e. (1) [X] Decedent died intestate.
   (2) [ ] Copy of decendent's will dated: [ ] codicils dated: are affixed as Attachment 3e (2)
      [ ] The will and all codicils are self-proving (Prob.code. §8220).

3. f. **Appointment of personal representative** (check all applicable boxes):

> Include in Attachment 3e(2) a typed copy of a handwritten will and a translation of a foreign language will.

  (1) Appointment of executor or administrator with will annexed:
    (a) [ ] Proposed executor is named as executor in the will and consents to act.
    (b) [ ] No executor is named in the will.
    (c) [ ] Proposed personal representative is a nominee of a person entitled to Letters. (Affix nomination as attachment 3f(1) (c).)
    (d) [ ] Other named executors will not act because of [ ] death [ ] declination [ ] other reasons (specify in Attachment 3f(1)(d).)
  (2) Appointment of administrator:
    (a) [X] Petitioner is a person entitled to Letters. (If necessary, explain priority in Attachment 3f(2)(a).)
    (b) [ ] Petitioner is a nominee of a person entitled to Letters. (Affix nomination as Attachment 3f(2)(b).)
    (c) [X] Petitioner is related to the decedent as (specify): SPOUSE
  (3) Appointment of special administrator requested. (Specify grounds and requested powers in Attachment 3f(3).)
  g. Proposed personal representative is a [X] resident of California [ ] nonresident of California (affix statement of permanent address as Attachment 3g) [X] resident of the United States [ ] nonresident of the United States.

4. [ ] Decedent's will does not preclude administration of this estate under the Independent Administration of Estates Act.

5. a.   The decedent is survived by (check at least one box in each of items (1)-(3))
    (1) [X] spouse [ ] no spouse as follows: [ ] divorced or never married [ ] spouse deceased
    (2) [X] child as follows: [X] natural or adopted [ ] natural adopted by a third party [ ] no child
    (3)   issue of a predeceased child [ ] no issue of a predeceased child
  b. Decedent [ ] is [X] is not   survived by a stepchild or foster child or children who would have been adopted by decedent but for a legal barrier. (See Prop. Code. §6454.)

6. (Complete if decedent was survived by (1) a spouse but no issue (only a or b apply), or (2) no spouse or issue. Check the first box that applies):
  a. [ ] Decedent is survived by a parent or parents who are listed in item 8.
  b. [ ] Decedent is survived by issue of deceased parents, all of whom are listed in item 8.
  c. [ ] Decedent is survived by a grandparent or grandparents who are listed in item 8.
  d. [ ] Decedent is survived by issue of grandparents, all of whom are listed in item 8.
  e. [ ] Decedent is survived by issue of predeceased spouse, all of whom are listed in item 8.
  f. [ ] Decedent is survived by next of kin, all of whom are listed in item 8.
  g. [ ] Decedent is survived by parents or a predeceased spouse or issue of those parents, if both are predeceased, all of whom are listed in item 8.
  h. [ ] Decedent is survived by no known next of kin.

7. (Complete only if no spouse or issue survived decedent) Decedent [ ] had no predeceased spouse [ ] had a predeceased spouse who (1) [ ] died not more than15 years before decedent owing an interest in **real property** that passed to decedent, (2) [ ] died not more than five years before decedent owning **personal property** valued at $10,000 or more that passed to decedent
  (3) [ ] neither (1) nor (2) apply. (if you checked (1) or (2), check only the first box that applies):
  a. [ ] Decedent is survived by issue of a predeceased spouse, all of whom are listed in item 8.
  b. [ ] Decedent is survived by a parent of parents of the predeceased spouse who are listed in item 8.
  c. [ ] Decedent is survived by issue of a parent of the predeceased spouse, all of whom are listed in item 8.
  d. [ ] Decedent is survived by next of kin of the decedent, all of whom are listed in item 8.
  e. [ ] Decedent is survived by next of kin of the predeceased spouse, all of whom are listed in item 8.

8. **Listed In Attachment 8** are the names, relationships, ages, and addresses, so far as known to or reasonably ascertainable by petitioner, of (1) all persons named in decedent's will and codicils, whether living or deceased, (2) all persons named or checked in items 2, 5, 6, and 7, and (3) all beneficiaries of a devisee trust in which the trustee and personal representative are the same person. ▶

9. Number of pages attached:1
  Date: 2 (7/ 9ʃ   (SIGNATURE OF ATTORNEY)

*(Signature of all petitioners also required (Prob. Code, S 1020).)

Exhibit 1.1 (Continued)

I declare under penalty of perjury under the laws of the State of California that the foregoing is true and correct.

Date: 2/17/5$

MARY BONO
_____
(TYPE OR PRINT NAME)

$\times$ ~~Mary Bono~~
(SIGNATURE OF PETITIONER)

_____
(TYPE OR PRINT NAME)

▶ _____
(SIGNATURE OF PETITIONER)

PETITION FOR PROBATE

Page two
CEB

ESTATE OF
SALVATORE PHILIP BONO

ATTACHMENT 8

Name and Address	Relationship	Age
Mary Bono 301 W. El Camino Way Palm Springs, CA 92264	Spouse	Adult
Chesare Bono 301 W. El Camino Way Palm Springs, CA 92264	Son	Minor Born 04/25/88
Chianna Bono 301 W. El Camino Way Palm Springs, CA 92264	Daughter	Minor Born 02/02/91
Chirsty Bono Fasce 18 64th Place Long Beach, CA 90803	Daughter	Adult
Chastity Bono 8968 Vista Grande Street Los Angeles, CA 90069	Daughter	Adult
Jean Bono 67834 Vega Road Cathedral City, CA 92234	Mother	Adult
Santo Bono 7981 Cleta Downey, CA 90241	Father	Adult
Fran Erickson 430 Benevente Drive Oceanside, CA 92057	Sister	Adult
Betty Oliva 10961 Harrogate Place Santa Ana, CA 92705	Sister	Adult

ATTORNEY OR PARTY WITHOUT ATTORNEY (*Name and Address*): 53606	TELEPHONE NO: (213) 629-4824

ATTORNEY OR PARTY WITHOUT ATTORNEY (*Name and Address*): 53606

Riordan & McKinzie
Jeffrey L. Glassman, Esq.
300 So. Grand Ave., #2900
Los Angeles, CA 90071
ATTORNEY FOR (*Name*): Afeni Shakur

TELEPHONE NO: (213) 629-4824

FOR COURT USE ONLY

FILED
LOS ANGELES SUPERIOR COURT

SEP 20 1996

JOHN A. CLARKE, CLERK
A. Arbertha
BY ALISHA ARBERTHA, DEPUTY

SUPERIOR COURT OF CALIFORNIA, COUNTY OF LOS ANGELES
STREET ADDRESS: 111 North Hill Street
MAILING ADDRESS:
CITY AND ZIP CODE: Los Angels, Ca 90012
BRANCH NAME: Central

ESTATE OF (*Name*): TUPAC A. SHAKUR,
aka TUPAC AMARU SHAKUR, aka TUPAC SHAKUR   DECEDENT

ORDER FOR PROBATE

ORDER
APPOINTING
- [ ] Executor
- [ ] Administrator with Will Annexed
- [ ] Administrator   [x] Special Administrator
- [ ] Order Authorizing Independent Administration of Estate
  - [ ] With full authority   [ ] with limited authority

CASE NUMBER:

BP042683

1. Date of hearing: 9/20/96   Dept/Rm: 11 45 AM   Time: 5   Judge: Robert J Blaylock Pro Tem

THE COURT FINDS

2. a. All notices required by law have been given.
   b. Decedent died on (*date*): 9/13/96
      (1) [x] a resident of the California county named above
      (2) [ ] a nonresident of California and left an estate in the county named above
   c. Decedent died
      (1) [x] intestate
      (2) [ ] testate and decedent's will dated:
          and each codicil dated:
          was admitted to probate by Minute Order on (*date*):

THE COURT ORDERS

3. (*Name*): Afeni Shakur
   is appointed personal representative:
   - a. [ ] Executor of the decedent's will
   - b. [ ] Administrator with will annexed
   - c. [ ] Administrator
   - d. [x] Special Administrator
     (1) [x] with special powers   *marshall assets*
     (2) [x] with special powers as specified marshall assets *Tac*
     (3) [x] without notice of hearing *Tac*

   and letters shall issue on qualification.

4. a. [ ] **Full authority** is granted to administer the estate under the Independent Administration of Estates Act.
   b. [ ] **Limited authority** is granted to administer the estate under the Independent Administration of Estates Act (there is no authority, without court supervision, to (1) sell or exchange real property or (2) grant an option to purchase real property or (3) borrow money with the loan secured by an encumbrance upon real property).

5. a. [ ] Bond is not required.
   b. [x] Bond is fixed at: $250,000.00   to be furnished by an authorized surety company or as otherwise provided by law.
   c. [ ] Deposits of: $ are ordered to be placed in a blocked account at (*specify institution and location*):
       and receipts shall be filed. No withdrawals shall be made without a court order.

6. [ ] (*Name*):   is appointed probate referee.
       Date:

   SEP 20 1996   ROBERT J. BLAYLOCK
                                      JUDGE OF THE SUPERIOR COURT   Pro Tem

7. [ ] Number of pages attached: Signature follows last attachment

Form Approved by the
Judicial Council of California
DE-140 (Rev. July 1. 1988)   **ORDER FOR PROBATE**   Probate Code, 329
                                                                                   CEB

Exhibit 1.2 Partial inventory from the estate of Tupac Shakur

Source: Tupac Shakur, Intestate, Case Number FP 042683, Superior Court of California, County of Los Angeles, Los Angeles, CA.

Estate of Tupac A. Shakur, Deceased
Case No. BP042683

Partial Inventory #1
Attachment 2

1.	55.371 shs Oppenheimer Account No. 230 2301277991 Strategic Income Fund A	322.26
2.	52.237 shs Oppenheimer Accont No. 300 3003396877 Equity Income Fund A	609.08
3.	Household furniture & furnishings	35,250.
4.	1995 Jaguar CV (XJS) SAJNX2741SC222099	45,000.
5.	1996 Hummer SW 137ZA8332TE170007	75,000.
6.	Rolex watch, president style, green dial, baguette bezel, oyster perpetual, diamond studded bracelet, 18K gold, 8 inches long. Total weight 460 full cut diamonds: 6.90 cts., baguettes: .96 cts., approx, total weight 8 cts.	17,500.
7.	Rolex bracelet, 18K gold, 7 ¾ inches long, style Rolex, 101 grams, diamond studded, 630 full cut diamonds, approx. total weight: 12.6 cts.	6,000.
8	Chain bracelet, 18K gold, 7 ¾ inches long, 750, weighting 102 grams, signed Gianni Versace, black enamel discs, diamond studded, approx. total weight: 3.5 cts.	5,000.
9.	Ruby, diamond bracelet, 14K gold, 9 inches long, 74 round rubies approx. total weight 3.6 cts., 258 full cut diamonds approx. total weight: 5.0 cts. (name plate on bracelet)	5,500.
10.	Diamond and 18K gold ring, 17 grams, approx. total diamond weight 5.15 cts.	4,000.

9

The 101 Biggest Estate Planning Mistakes

Estate of Tupac A. Shakur, Deceased
Case No. BP042683

Partial Inventory #1
Attachment 2

11. 2PAC 14 gold and diamond ring, 2.10 cts., approx. total weight 24.8 grams — 2,000

12. Diamond solitaire ring, 14K gold amount weighting 16.2 grams with approx. total weight 3.1 cts. round brilliant cut diamond — 8,250.

13. Diamond stud earring, 14K, approx. weight 2.00 cts. — 4,500.

14. Diamond stud earring, 14K, approx weight .03 cts. — 50.

Exhibit 1.2 (*Continued*)

IN THE SUPREME COURT OF JUDICATURE OF JAMAICA

IN PROBATE AND ADMINISTRATION

> IN THE ESTATE of ROBERT NESTA
> MARLEY late of 56 Hope Road,
> Kingston 6, in the Parish of
> Saint Andrew, Musician & Entertainer
> deceased, intestate.

    A TRUE DECLARATION of all and singular the estate and effects of ROBERT NESTA MARLEY late of 56 Hope Road, Kingston 6, in the Parish of Saint Andrew, Musician & Entertainer deceased intestate, who died on the 11th day of May, 1981 which have at any time since his death come to the hands possession or knowledge of RITA MARLEY, GEORGE DESNOES, and THE ROYAL BANK TRUST COMPANY (JAMAICA) LIMITED the Administrators made and exhibited upon the corporal oath of the said RITA MARLEY GEORGE DESNOES and GEORGE LOUIS DUNCAN BYLES one of the Officers of The Royal Bank Trust Company (Jamaica) Limited duly authorised to make this oath on behalf of the Bank as follows to wit:-

FIRSTLY: These Declarants say that the deceased was at the time of his death possessed of or entitled to the following Personal Estate:-

Shares in:	Tuff Gong Records Limited	)	
	Tuff Gong Recording Studio Limited	))	$1,500,000.00
	Addis Manufacturing Company Limited	))	
	Cash in Bank		50,000.00
	Motor Vehicles		100,000.00
			$1,650,000.00

Exhibit 1.3 Jamaican court papers for the estate of Bob Marley

Source: Bob Marley, Intestate, Suit Number P533 of 1981, The Supreme Court of Judicature, Kingston, Jamaica.

SECONDLY: These Declarants say that the deceased was at the time of. his death possessed of or entitled to the following Real Estate:-

Premises at 56 Hope Road
Kingston 6, in the Parish
of Saint Andrew
valued at $400,000.00

LASTLY: These Declarants further say that No Estate of or.belonging to the said deceased have at any time since his death come to the hands possession or knowledge of these Declarants save as hereinbefore set forth.

SWORN to by the said RITA MARLEY   )
at   4 Duke Street   )
in the Parish of   Kingston   )   _Rita Marley_
this 27thday of October   )
1981, before me:-   )

            Justice of the Peace
            for the Parish of:- Kingston

SWORN to by the said GEORGE   )
DESNOES at   4 Duke Street   )
in the Parish of   Kingston   ):   _George Desnoes_
this 27th day of October   )
1981, before me:-   )

            Justice of the Peace

Exhibit 1.3 (*Continued*)

are able to make a Will that does not benefit them "disappear." Sometimes Wills are lost when a lawyer moves offices and files are misplaced as a result.

There are alternatives to making a Last Will and Testament. You can establish a trust during your lifetime that owns all of your property; that property is instantly transferred upon your death to the remaindermen of such a trust. Such a trust can avoid the court procedure by which a Will is proved to be valid or invalid to the satisfaction of the probate or surrogate's court judge. The word *probate* comes from the word *probatio*, which in the canon law consisted of the proof of a Will by an executor.

In the end, those who fail to plan, plan to fail. Those words are so true when it comes to estate planning. Therefore, the first, and most critical estate planning mistake, is simply failing to plan.

Mistake #2: **Out-of-Date Wills**

Despite having been the Attorney General of the United States of America, Robert F. ("Bobby") Kennedy left a Last Will and Testament that was obviously out of date. Signed in 1953, Bobby's Last Will and Testament[2] named his brother, John F. Kennedy, as a co-executor, co-trustee and successor guardian of his and his wife, Ethel's, numerous minor children. The other named co-executor was Bobby's youngest brother, Edward "Teddy" Kennedy. Unfortunately, despite the assassination of his brother and co-executor, President John F. Kennedy in 1963, Bobby Kennedy never updated his Will to reflect that fact. This might have proved quite problematic when Bobby was assassinated just five years later in 1968.

Fortunately, though, Bobby's Will was properly drafted and provided for the contingency that if any of the named executors did not act, then the following persons, in the order named, were designated to fill any vacancy: Eunice Kennedy Shriver, Patricia Kennedy Lawford, and Jean Kennedy Smith.

The probate papers filed with the New York County Surrogate's Court indicated that sister Eunice renounced her right to act as a successor executor.[3] Consequently, it was sister Patricia Lawford who filled the void left by John's death. That decision does not seem to have been the result of any disharmony in the family, as Eunice was living in Paris, France at the time and Patricia lived on Fifth Avenue in New York City.

Given that Bobby was a lawyer, it seems odd that he didn't change his Will after John was killed in 1963. This failure to update might seem even more surprising because Bobby was not just any attorney, but none other than the Attorney General of the United States of America. In my own law practice, I have noticed over the years that lawyers (other than those specializing in trusts and estates matters) are often quite delinquent in keeping their own estate planning documents current. Perhaps Bobby, like most busy attorneys, put his personal affairs last.

At the time of his assassination in 1968, Bobby had 10 children, and his wife, Ethel, was pregnant with another daughter. Rory Elizabeth Katharine Kennedy was born five months after her father's death. It is yet another sad footnote to the tragic history of the Kennedy family that on the day of Rory's wedding, her cousin, John F. Kennedy, Jr., his wife, and his sister-in-law died when their plane crashed into the sea.

The horrific death and divorce of Wall Street mogul R. Theodore ("Ted") Ammon is also an example of the ramifications of failing to keep one's Will current, particularly given the changing marital circumstances in people's often tumultuous lives. Despite going through an unusually ugly and bitter divorce, the multimillionaire wonder boy never updated the Will that he had signed on August 22, 1995, before the end of his marriage and his life.

Ted Ammon's Will had been prepared by one of New York City's fanciest and finest (i.e., most expensive) law firms, Skadden, Arps, Slate, Meager & Flom, and was a whopping 45 pages long.[4] The Will provided that Ammon's wife, Generosa, was to be a co-executor with the venerable bank, J.P. Morgan Chase & Company. Generosa was also the named beneficiary of all of Ammon's tangible personal property, real estate, interests in Kohlberg Kravis Roberts & Co., and almost the entire residuary estate, either outright or in trust. Generosa would have been entitled to none of that after the divorce was completed, but it never was. At the time of Ted Ammon's murder in his mansion in East Hampton, New York on October 22, 2001, he was still legally married to Generosa, and his Will, which gave her almost everything, was valid and admitted to probate, but badly and sadly out of date.

One has to wonder what Mr. Ammon and his high-priced lawyers were thinking when they never updated his Will despite his impending and bitter divorce. We can only speculate as to whether the fact that the Will was not ever changed was one of the motivating factors leading to Ted Ammon's murder by an electrician named Danny Pelosi. Mr. Pelosi married Generosa Ammon about three months after her husband's death. Mr. Pelosi was convicted of the murder of Ted Ammon and is serving a life sentence in jail, and Generosa Ammon Pelosi died from breast cancer in 2005. Mrs. Pelosi did not make the same mistake as her former husband Ted; in her last Last Will and Testament, she made no provisions for her surviving husband, jailbird Danny Pelosi.

Mistake #3: Losing Your Will

L et's face it. We all lose something sometimes. However, when the thing that is lost is a Last Will and Testament, then that loss can have serious implications that could cost your estate additional taxes and throw the proverbial monkey wrench into your estate plan. People don't plan to lose things, but despite that, it still happens all the time.

This begs the question, "Where is the best place for me to keep my Will?" Most experienced trusts and estates attorneys would agree that it is best if the client does *not* keep his or her original Will, and if the client does keep it, that he or she does not put it in a safe deposit box at a bank to which he or she is the only person with access to that box. For practical reasons, if the client keeps his or her Will and is the only one who knows that the Will is in the shoe-box in the guestroom closet, then that Will may never be located. If the client feels that the shoebox is not secure enough and puts the Will in a safe deposit box in the vault at a bank, that box may be sealed and be inaccessible once the client has died. Even if you have given someone else a power of attorney with authority to access your safe deposit box, that power of attorney terminates when the principal dies, and the agent may be left out in the cold. It may require a court order to allow someone to access that safe deposit to search for your Will, and obtaining that court order may be time consuming and expensive.

The best place to leave your Last Will and Testament is with the attorney who prepared it. Just be sure that he or she sends you a conformed copy or photocopy of your Will shortly after you have signed it. Under New York law, and in many other states as well, if the original Will was in possession of the client and the Will cannot be located after the client dies, it is presumed that the client revoked that Will, and the estate may pass by intestacy or by the terms of a prior Will. If the attorney keeps the original Will in his or her possession, then no such presumption arises, and a copy of the Will may then be admitted to probate if the original cannot be located.

Although I have never lost the original Will of a client of mine, I have seen many cases where that has happened, especially around the time that an attorney might be retiring or closing down his practice. That is often when client files, including original documents such as a Last Will and Testament, get lost in a big dumpster. It is irresponsible and unprofessional behavior for the attorney not to protect and preserve his client's important documents, but it happens nonetheless. The appropriate action would be to file the client's original Will with the surrogate's court for safekeeping or to obtain the client's permission and instructions to send the original Will to another attorney who will be representing that client in the future. Returning an original Will to the client is not generally a good idea for all of the reasons listed above. To avoid this happening to you, it is a good idea to stay in touch with your attorney and be sure that he or she always has current contact information for you.

Regardless, it is a mistake for the client to insist on holding his or her original Will, because at the time that the Will is needed, the client is no longer anywhere to be found.

Mistake # 4: **Do-It-Yourselfers and Handwritten Wills**

Many people adhere to the belief that if you want a job done right, you need to do it yourself. That applies to people who are not lawyers, but believe that they can do a better job than a lawyer even if they don't have a legal degree. Some people believe that lawyers just "get in the way" of communication, and they prefer to take written matters into their own hands. Sometimes that can be fine, but oftentimes, trying to write your Will without legal advice is a prescription for disaster.

From California, the land of fruits, flakes, and nuts, we get the following two handwritten (i.e., holographic) Wills of comedian Phil Silvers (Exhibit 1.4) and film director John Cassavetes (Exhibit 1.5), who died in Los Angeles, California in 1985 and 1989, respectively.

Whereas these two holographic Wills with no witnesses, which are reproduced in Exhibit 1.4 and 1.5, could be and were in fact probated in the State of California, the same would not be true in the State of New York and many others. In California, the signature and material portions of a Will must be handwritten by the testator to be deemed acceptable; however, New York courts will not accept holographic Wills, except for those of military personnel or persons serving with or accompanying them. Although Phil Silvers may have been Sergeant Bilko on the tube, he was not serving in the military at the time that he scrawled out his Will in his own scratchy handwriting. For ease of reading, Silvers' Will appears in its original handwritten form in Exhibit1.4a and is transcribed in Exhibit 1.4b.

Although Silvers actually wrote his Will while he was in New York, it was probated in California. As much as people may have liked Phil Silvers' shtick, he was not a preparer of legal documents. Silvers ends his Will with the single Hebrew word "Shalom," which

Phil Silvers

This handwritten document (July 4th 1984)
will serve as my last will and testament
I request for David Flynn of the firm of Treubner T Flynn
to share the duties of Executor with my eldest daughter Tracey
For carrying out my requests they are to receive and
share the sum of Five Thousand dollars $5000 each
— Executing the following requests I leave my entire fortune
To be shared equally by my five daughters namely

Tracey, Nancy, Cathy, Candace and Jaury, This legacy include
my ownerships of all Stocks and Bonds, Bank accounts, securities
and monies in banks and possible partial ownership such as
the Television series "Gilligan Island" — My many awards and
documents, photos, and memorabilia should be shared equally
by my five above mentioned daughters, this is to be supervised
by my eldest child Tracey

my further request
To my sister mrs Pearl Saben of 280 W 59th St New York City
x 10019
the Sum of Fifteen Thousand dollars $15,000

To my brother Bob Silver 1130 Brighton Beach Ave
Brooklyn, N.Y. 11235
Fifteen thousand dollars $1500
In the event both the above my sister and sister are not alive to
accept this legacy both Sums $30,000 Thirty thousand in total
should be awarded my Nephew Saul Silver
390 First Ave

Exhibit 1.4a An excerpt from the handwritten Will of Phil Silvers

Source: Phil Silvers, Will dated July 4, 1984, proved November 15, 1985, Case Number P 703086, Superior Court of California, County of Los Angeles, Los Angeles, CA.

The Single Biggest Mistake Is Not Planning

Phil Silvers

(July 4th 1984)

This handwritten document
will serve as my last will and testament
I request for David Flynn of the firm of Traubner & Flynn to share the duties of Executor with my eldest daughter Tracey
    For carrying out my requests they are to receive and share the sum of Five thousand dollars $2500 each
    Excuding the following bequests I leave my entire fortune to be shares equally by my five daughters namely
Tracey, Nancey, Cathy, Candance and Laury. This legacy includes my ownerships of all Stock and Bodns, Bank accounts, securities and monies in banks and possible partial ownerships such as the television series "Gilligan Island" – My many awards and documents, photos, and memophilia should be shared equally by my five above mentioned daughters, this is to be supervised by my eldest child Tracey
    My further requests
To my sister Mrs. Pearl Sabin of 200 W 54th St New York City
        10014
the sum of Fifteen Thousand dollars $15,000
    To my brother Bob Silver 1120 Brighter Beach Ave
        Brooklyn, N.Y
          11235
Fifteen thousand dollars $1500
In the event both the above my Brother and Sister are not alive to accept this legacy both Sums $30,000 Thirty thousand in Total should be awarded my Nephew Saul Silver
        390 First Ave
          New York City
            N.Y. 10010

Exhibit 1.4b A transcribed excerpt of the handwritten Will of Phil Silvers

means hello, goodbye, and peace. As Silvers says in his Will, he was "one of a kind," and so was his Will.

The blunt, no-nonsense style of film director John Cassavetes comes through loud and clear in his one-page Will, which is reproduced in its entirety in Exhibit 1.5. Cassavetes' wife of 30 years, actress Gena Rowlands, was appointed the executor of her husband's handwritten Will by the Superior Court of California, Los Angeles County.

ATTACHMENT 4

June 3, 1988

I, John Cassavetes, being of sound mind, and living at 7917 Woodrow Wilson Drive Los Angeles 90046. Cal. do hereby declare My Last Will and Testament as follows:

I leave all and every thing I own or will own to my beloved wife. Gena Rowlands Cassavetes.

I leave nothing to anyone else, whomsoever, they may be.

I owe noone any debt or obligation, other than usual and ordinary bills.

No one has done me a special service that I feel obligated to.

I hereby appoint my wife, Gena Executor of this will. She may at her discretion appoint another executor.

John Cassavetes
June 3, 1988

This document, my only valid will replaces any previous will that might have been drawn. and has been witnessed by my attorney, James Cohen. and my secretary, Doe Aredon Siegel bothof Los Angeles, Cal. Enclosed their witness document. - Jt John Cassavetes June 3, 1988 —

Exhibit 1.5 The complete handwritten Will of John Cassavetes

Source: John Cassavetes, Will dated June 3, 1988, proved April 2, 1989, Case Number P. 732515, Superior Court of California, County of Los Angeles, Los Angeles, CA.

Cassavetes's handwritten Will was witnessed by his attorney and his secretary, but it is pure Cassavetes that states, "I owe no one any debt or obligation . . . "

Although Silvers and Cassavetes are amusing examples of hand-written Wills that worked, there are many more stories of handwritten Wills that did not work. If your Will is not accepted as valid by a court of law, your estate will be distributed by the governing laws of intestacy, instead of in accordance with your own wishes. Unless you are Phil Silvers or John Cassavetes, or you follow the proper legal procedures in the state you are in, it is a mistake to handwrite your own Will and attempt to execute it, especially without legal advice.

Mistake #5: Not Signing Your Will because You Physically Can't

Accidents happen. Just ask Superman, Christopher Reeve, whose body was completely paralyzed at the age of 42 as the result of breaking his neck in a freak horseback riding accident. Reeves' paralysis was so bad that he could not even sign his name, although he still he had his mental faculties up until the day he died on October 10, 2004, almost 10 years after his tragic fall.

When Reeve "signed" his Last Will and Testament on September 15, 2003, he could not in fact write his name or even grip a pen or pencil to make an "X." Instead, Reeve was correctly advised to take advantage of the provisions of New York's Estates, Powers and Trusts law Section 3-2.1, which provides that a valid Will may be signed "in the name of the testator, by another person in his presence and by his direction." Thus, Reeve's wife, Dana Morosini Reeve, not only signed her husband's name and her name on the signature page of his Will reproduced in Exhibit 1.6, but she also put his initials on each and every preceding page of his Will.

The following two (see Exhibit 1.7 and 1.8) affidavits signed by Dana Morosini Reeve state exactly how the Will was executed at her husband's express direction. These affidavits were obviously prepared by experienced legal counsel who knew the requirements of New York State law, as the paralyzed Reeve obviously needed good legal advice on the question of how a paralyzed person can properly execute a valid Last Will and Testament.

There are similar unusual requirements for the due execution of a Will when the testator is blind. Take the composer, singer, performer, and musician Ray Charles, for example. Perhaps the most famous blind man of the twentieth century, Ray Charles had Joe Adams, his business manager, longtime friend, and the executor of

The Single Biggest Mistake Is Not Planning

for my Last Will and Testament. And have hereunto set my hand and seal, all this *15ᵗʰ* day of *September.* 2003.

Christopher Reeve

CHRISTOPHER REEVE

Dana Morosini Reeve

DANA MOROSINI REEVE

Address,
11 Great Hill Farms Road
Bedford, NY 10506

     The foregoing instrument, consisting of fifteen pages, was signed, sealed, published and declared by CHRISTOPHER REEVE, the above-named Testator, (who directed his wife, Dana Morosini Reeve, to sign said document on his behalf), as and for his Last Bedford. NY 10506, all being present at the same time, and thereupon we, at his request and his presence and in presence of each other, have hereunto subscribed our names as witnesses, all this *15ᵗʰ* day of *SEPTEMBER* 2003.

DOLORES ARRO	residing at	349 BEDFORD CTR. RD.
Dano		BEDFORD HILLS N Y 10507
LAURIE HAWKINS	residing at	3165 29ᵗʰ St #D4
Le. Harkins		Astoria, ny 11106
JEMA CHEUNG	residing at	81 THORNDIKE ST. #B
Cheung...		BROOKLINE, MA 02446

Exhibit 1.6 Excerpt from the Will of Christopher Reeve

Source: Christopher Reeve, Will dated September 15, 2003, proved November 22, 2004, File Number 3161-2004, Surrogate's Court, County of Westchester, White Plains, NY.

his Will, sign Charles's signature for him in front of two subscribing witnesses.[5] One of those witnesses, Peter L. Funsten, was named as successor executor of the Will and was also the attorney who prepared the Last Will and Testament of Ray Charles.

AFFIDAVIT

    Each of the undersigned, individually and severally, being duly sworn, deposes and says:

    The within Last Will and Testament was initialed and signed on behalf of Christopher Reeve by his wife, Dana Morosini Reeve, in our presence and sight on the/5 ITbay of September 2003 at 11 Great Hill Farms Road, Bedford, NY 10506. Christopher Reeve did not initial and sign said Power of Attorney because at the time he was physically unable to do so. Each of the undersigned witnessed Christopher Reeve clearly and unequivocally direct Dana Morosini Reeve to execute the Will on his behalf. Christopher Reeve, at the time of directing Dana Morosini Reeve to execute said Will on his behalf, declared the instrument so subscribed to be his Last Will and Testament. Each of the undersigned thereupon signed his or her name as a witness on the Will, at the request of Christopher Reeve and in his presence and sight and in the presence and sight of each other.

    Christopher Reeve was, at the time of directing the execution of his Will, over the age of eighteen years and, in the respective opinions of the undersigned, of sound mind, memory and understanding and, other than his physical disability, not under any restraint or in any respect incompetent to make a Last Will and Testament.

    Each of the undersigned was acquainted with Christopher Reeve at such time, and makes this affidavit at his request. Each of the undersigned was also acquainted with Dana Morosini Reeve at such time, and witnessed her initial and sign the Will at Christopher Reeve's direction and on his behalf. The within Will was shown to the undersigned at the time this affidavit was made, and was examined by each of them as to the signature of the Testator (as signed by Dana Morosini Reeve), as to the signature of Dana Morosini Reeve, and as to the signatures of the undersigned.

Severally sworn to before me
this _15_ day of _September_, 2003.

TRACEY E. JENKINS
Nota...

Exhibit 1.7 Affidavit of attesting witnesses to the Will of Christopher Reeve

Source: Christopher Reeve, Will dated September 15, 2003, proved November 22, 2004, File Number 3161-2004, Surrogate's Court, County of Westchester, White Plains, NY.

AFFIDAVIT

DANA MOROSINI REEVE, being duly sworn, deposes and says:

On SEPTEMBER 15, 2003, I initialed and signed the within Will on behalf of my husband, Christopher Reeve, at his specific direction and request. Christopher Reeve did not initial and sign said Power of Attorney himself because at the time he was physically unable to do so.

Christopher Reeve directed me to place his initials on each of the pages of the Will, and to sign his name on the signature line on page 15 of the Last Will and Testament. At the time that Christopher Reeve directed me to execute said Will on his behalf, he clearly understood and stated that the document was his Last Will and Testament. I initialed and signed the Will in the presence and sight of Christopher Reeve and in the presence and sight of numerous persons, three of whom have signed their names to the Last Will and Testament as witnesses. Pursuant to Section 3-2.1(a)(1)(C) of the Estate, Powers and Trusts Law, I also signed my own name and affixed my residence address to page 15 of the Will.

Christopher Reeve was, at the time of directing me to initial and sign his Last Will and Testament, over the age of eighteen years and of sound mind, memory and understanding and, other than his physical disability, not under any restraint or in any respect incompetent to make a Last Will and Testament.

DANA MOROSINI REEVE

Sworn to before me this
15 day of SEPTEMBER, 2003.

Notary Public

Exhibit 1.8 Affidavit of Dana Morosini Reeve

Source: Christopher Reeve, Will dated September 15, 2003, proved November 22, 2004, File Number 3161-2004, Surrogate's Court, County of Westchester, White Plains, NY.

Interestingly, neither the Will of Ray Charles nor any of the attachments to it state that the testator was totally blind and was directing that his Will be signed by someone else. New York's Estates, Powers and Trusts Law Section 3-2.1(a)(1)(c) is quite specific about the procedures required when a blind person signs his or her Will. At the very least, the Will being signed should be read in its entirety to the blind testator. Every state has its own rules and laws about the necessary legal procedures. The applicable California statute on the subject is much looser, as many things in California are, than the applicable New York statute. In any case, the Will of Ray Charles was admitted to probate by the Superior Court of California, County of Los Angeles, so whatever Charles and Adams did, it worked.

Finally, we should not forget The Great One, Jackie Gleason, who died a resident of the State of Florida. Gleason's legal name was Herbert John Gleason at his birth in Brooklyn, New York in 1916, and his name was the same at his death on June 24, 1987. Most interesting about Gleason's Will is not the Will itself, but the first codicil to that Will, which he signed literally the day before he died. In that codicil, Gleason increased a bequest to his longtime secretary Sydell Spear from $25,000 to $100,000. Because he was near death, Gleason was not able to sign the codicil himself, but instead directed another person to do so for him in the presence of two witnesses. Jackie Gleason's first, and last, codicil is reproduced partially in Exhibit 1.9.

Life's slings and arrows can cause a person to suffer from paralysis, blindness, or other debilitating illness that could preclude a person from signing his or her name. However, laws have been created that establish legal procedures to be sure that your Will is duly executed, even if you can't sign it yourself, as we see in the cases of Christopher Reeve and Jackie Gleason. It is a mistake not to have the benefit of knowledgeable legal counsel if you are attempting to execute your Will but are not able to sign it.

FIRST CODICIL TO LAST WILL AND TESTAMENT

OF

HERBERT JOHN GLEASON

I, HERBERT JOHN GLEASON, also known as JACKIE GLEASON, a resident of the State of Florida, being of sound mind and memory, do hereby make, publish and declare this to be a Codicil to my Last Will and Testament of April 11, 1985.

FIRST: I hereby delete Article IV of my said Last Will and Testament, and I hereby substitute therefor the following new Article IV:

IV. I give and bequeath to my longtime secretary SYDELL SPEAR, if she survives me, the sum of One Hundred Thousand ($100,000) Dollars. If SYDELL SPEAR shall fail to survive me, the gift and bequest under this Article IV shall lapse.

SECOND: I hereby delete subparagraph (A) (i) of Article V of my said Last Will and Testament, and I hereby substitute therefor the following new subparagraph (A) (i):

(A) (i) If my wife MARILYN GLEASON shall survive me and any child of mine or any descendant of a child of mine shall also survive me, then I give, devise and bequeath an

1

Exhibit 1.9 Excerpt from the First Codicil to the Will of Jackie Gleason
Source: Jackie Gleason, Will dated April 11, 2985, proved July 6, 1987, File Number 87-442, Circuit Court, Broward County, Fort Lauderdale, FL.

and confirm my Last Will and Testament of April 11, 1985.

IN WITNESS WHEREOF, I, the undersigned testator, have on this 23ᴰ day of *June* , 1987, signed, sealed, published and declared this instrument as and for a codicil to my Last Will and Testament of April 11, 1985 in the presence of *Richard G. Green* and *Irwin D. Marks* whom I have requested to become attesting witnesses hereto.

Herbert John Gleason (L.S.)

HERBERT JOHN GLEASON

On *June 23d*, 1987, and in our presence the foregoing instrument consisting of this and three preceding typewritten pages was declared by Herbert John Gleason to be a Codicil to his Last Will and Testament of April 11, 1985, and his name was subscribed at the end of the Codicil by *Richard G Green* in the testator's presence and by his direction and in our presence. We have this 23 day of *June* 1987 subscribed our names as witnesses in the presence of the testator and at his request and in the presence of each other after the testator's name was subscribed by *Richard G Green* by the direction of Herbert John Gleason.

_____ residing at *2065 North Bayrd Miami Beach, Florida*

_____ residing at *205 Yorktown Court Washington Township NJ 07675*

STATE OF FLORIDA
COUNTY OF BROWARD

We, Herbert John Gleason, *Brian P. Patchen*, and *Irwin D Marks*, the testator and the witnesses respectively, whose names are signed to the foregoing instrument, having been sworn, declared to the undersigned officer that the testator

Exhibit 1.9 *(Continued)*

30

The Single Biggest Mistake Is Not Planning

witnesses, directed ___RICHARD G GREEN___ to sign
for him his name to the foregoing instrument as a Codicil
to his Last Will and Testament of April 11, 1985, and that
each of the witnesses, in the presence of the testator and
in the presence of each other, signed the codicil as a
witness.

Herbert John Gleason
Testator

[signature]
Witness

[signature]
Witness

Subscribed and sworn to before me by Herbert John
Gleason, the testator, whose name was signed at his
direction by ___RICHARD G GREEN___, and by
___BRIAN P PATCHEN___ and ___ERWIN D. MARKS___,
the witnesses, on ___June 23___, 1987.

Adrienne Parkinson
Notary Public
My Commission Expires

Mistake #6 Not Properly Executing Documents

There have been numerous occasions over the years where a client of ours has called and said that he or she is going away soon, and needs to sign his or her Will before boarding a plane bound for Tanzania, Hong Kong, or some other far away land. Unfortunately, he explains, he and his wife cannot come to our office to sign the documents, and would prefer that we send them to them to get everything signed. I patiently explain that it is not that simple to properly execute a Will (ask Howard Hughes), and that there are important legal reasons that a Will should be signed under a lawyer's supervision and preferably in a lawyer's office.

Every state has its own legal requirements for a Will to be properly and duly executed, and those requirements must be observed or the Will will fail to be admitted to probate by any Court that has jurisdiction. The proper execution of a Will requires certain specific statutory formalities, involving two or three witnesses, affidavits, and/or a Notary Public. Every state has its own law on this subject. However, regardless of what the state law provides, the requirements need to be met precisely; if they are not, a Will can be denied probate because it was not properly executed.

A lawyer who specializes in Wills and estates would be expected to know all of the appropriate formalities and "magic words" that are necessary to have a Will duly executed. In New York, signing a Will in a lawyer's office under a lawyer's supervision leads to a "presumption of regularity," which could be determinative as to whether a Will is denied or admitted to probate.

I was involved in a Will contest involving the purported Will of a well-known international art dealer named Max Hutchinson who had essentially abandoned his wife and children in Australia and was involved with a woman from New York at the time he died. After he died, the Will was offered for probate in the Sullivan County Surrogate's Court. The problem with the purported Will was that the decedent's girlfriend was not only a beneficiary named in the purported Will, but she was also one of the witnesses to it. *Big* mistake, for her, but lucky break for the family.

Not only did having girlfriend Marion Kaselle acting as a witness void and nullify the bequests made to her under the purported Will, but the alleged Will itself was never admitted to probate. If that purported Will had been signed in a lawyer's office, any trusts and estates lawyer worth his or her salt would never let a beneficiary act as a witness. If a lawyer did allow that kind of a mistake to happen, he might be liable for legal malpractice, or at best be the object of the ire of the disinherited witness/beneficiary.

When it comes to signing a Will, don't be penny wise and pound foolish. Be sure to sign your Will under the supervision of an attorney who specializes in the fields of Wills, estates, and trusts.

The problem of clients taking legal matters into their own hands has been exacerbated in the Internet age. Clients often ask if they can have their Last Wills and Testaments sent to them as an electronic file over the Internet. Not only am I uncomfortable sending such important documents to clients online, based on privacy and confidentiality concerns, but I also believe that putting the document in the client's computer may tempt, and empower, a non-lawyer client to edit his or her Will in the future, in a manner that could be problematic. It also tempts the clients to sign his or her Will without being sure it is done properly under the supervision of an attorney.

On those occasions where the client absolutely cannot get to an attorney's office to sign the Will, we have sent written instructions similar to those shown in Exhibit 1.10 for our New York clients to assist them with the proper execution of their Wills.

And despite our best efforts in this regard, the Wills sent to clients, and then signed by clients without a lawyer supervising the Will execution, are usually returned with some ridiculous defect or mistake that requires that those Wills be signed again. But hopefully, the next time they do it in my office under my experienced supervision.

INSTRUCTIONS FOR EXECUTION OF A WILL
(without a supervising attorney)

1. Gather three adults who are neither beneficiaries under the will nor related to the Testator.

2. <u>Testator should</u>:

   (a) Place his initials, in pen, in the lower right margin of each page of the Will;

   (b) Fill in the date in the "IN WITNESS WHEREOF" paragraph at the end of the Will and then sign his name (<u>exactly</u> as written) on the line following that paragraph; and then.

   (c) Turn to the three witnesses and say "I hereby declare the instrument which you have seen me sign to be my Last Will land Testament, and I hereby request all of you to act as my witnesses."

3. <u>Witnesses</u>:

   (a) One of the witnesses should read aloud the paragraph which follows the line on which the Testator has signed his name. That witness should then, on the line following and on the attached affidavit, sign his or her name and include his or her residence address where indicated.

   (b) The other two witnesses should then sign their names and fill in their residence addresses on the Will, <u>and</u> sign the attached affidavit.

   (c) All three witnesses should print their names on the lines provided at the top of the affidavit and one of the witnesses should also write the street address and city where the Will was executed on the line provided in Paragraph 1 of the affidavit.

4. <u>Notary Public</u>:

   The witnesses should acknowledge their signatures on the affidavit before a Notary Public and the Notary should then place his or her signature and Notary Public stamp on the affidavit. The Notary Public should also include the date and place of signing where indicated in Paragraph 1 of the affidavit.

****

The testator and all witnesses should remain in the same room throughout the foregoing ceremony; none of them should leave the room until all have witnessed the Will. Only the original of the Will should be signed by the testator and the witnesses. A conformed copy of the original will should be prepared and kept in a secure place separate from the original instrument. The original will should be returned to the attorney draftsman as soon as possible.

<u>Note</u>: The staples in the Will should never, under any circumstances, be removed, not even for photocopying.

Exhibit 1.10 Instructions for the execution of a Will in New York without a supervising attorney

---

Mistake #7: The Best-Laid (Estate) Plans

Imagine that you are one of the world's richest men. A tad bit eccentric and irreverent, you don't want people to know who (or what) you are planning to leave your vast fortune to when you die. What do you do? What don't you do? Billionaire Howard Hughes, who died in 1976, might have thought that he had a good answer to these questions.

At the time of his death, Hughes had been divorced twice, most recently in 1971, and was not survived by any children. The multiple legal proceedings surrounding Hughes' huge estate took place in courts in Texas, Nevada, and California. At the end of the proverbial day, not one of the 30 purported Wills of Howard Hughes that had been offered for probate was ever admitted to probate by any court.

Following are copies of only three of the many purported Wills of Howard Hughes. (See Exhibits 1.11, 1.12, and 1.13) The first one was allegedly handwritten by Hughes, and it leaves his entire estate to the Howard Hughes Medical Institute, which he had created in 1953. If all of his property had actually passed to a charitable organization such as the HHMI, there would not have been any estate taxes payable as a result of the unlimited charitable deduction that would have been available to Hughes' estate, and medical research would have benefited as a result.

The next purported Will, which is reproduced in Exhibit 1.12 in its entirety, states that Hughes "leaves" his entire estate to "my son, Richard Robard Hughes, aka Joseph Michael Brown." Unfortunately for Mr. Brown, paternity was never established, and his claim to the entire Hughes fortune was rejected.

Finally, there is the well-known "Melvin Dummar/Mormon Church" version of Howard Hughes' purported Last Will and Testament (Exhibit 1.13), which was referred to in the film *Melvin*

Jan. 11/72

This is my last will and testament.

(1) I hereby revoke all wills and testamentary dispositions of every nature or kind whatsoever made by me before this date.

(2) I nominate, constitute, and appoint my counsel Chester C. Davis, sole executor and trustee of this, my last will, and testament. I refer to my executor and trustee in this document from this point forward as the "trustee".

(3) I give, devise, and bequeath all my monies, holdings, property of every nature and kind, all of my possessions and any profits of the before mentioned to the Howard Hughes Medical Institute for the use of medical research and the betterment of medical and health standards around the world.

(4) I hereby direct my trustee Chester Davis and my assistants Nadine Henley and Frank Gay to continue in their positions and duties, and to also assume a controlling interest in management in the Medical Institute, to decide, direct and implement policies and funds for the proper uses of the Medical Institute in the areas of medical research and the betterment of world health and medical standards.

(5) I hereby request that my trustee make known to any business associates, aides, or confidantes who wish to, or have undertaken a written documentation of any or all parts of my life, the terms of the Rosemont Enterprises agreement and possible infringements thereof - because of the conditions of that document.

(6) I hereby direct my trustee to instruct Rosemont Enterprises to complete all written, visual, and audio, documentation in the presentation of the factual representation of my life for public release two years to the day, after my death.

(7) I authorize my trustee to make funds available limited to one quarter of my total estate to a private agency of my trustee's choice, in the event of my death by unnatural or man-made cause; to apprehend such person or group of persons and to bring them within full prosecution of the law; the funds being made available for legal expenses and costs incurred on behalf of the trustee's appointed agency.

EXHIBIT "C"

Exhibit 1.11 Howard Hughes's Will: The Howard Hughes Medical Institute version

Source: Howard Hughes, Will dated June 11, 1972, Will not probated.

---

(8) I wish to make known to my trustee that I did not at any time enter into any contracts, agreements, or promises either oral or written, that transferred gave or bequeathed the bulk or any part of my estate to any person, persons, organizations or whatever other than the Howard Hughes Medical Institute. I sign this as my last will and testament.

Howard R. Hughes
Jan. 11, 1972

Exhibit 1.11 (*Continued*)

LAST WILL AND TESTAMENT
OF
HOWARD ROBARD HUGHES, JR.

I, Howard Robard Hughes, being of sound mind and body do hereby declare this my last will and testament. I leave my entire estate to my son, Richard Robard Hughes, aka Joseph Michael Brown, born September, 12th, 1945 in Fort Worth, Texas. At this time, I plan to make public my son's existence but in the event I am unable to do that, this will cannel and supercede any previous wills that I have made in the past. By the time this would be read attorneys for Summa Corporation should have approached my son but in the event that has not been done my son should request a full accounting of all my holdings and should take full control thereof.

Howard T Hughes

Grover Albert Walker

WITNESS

Donald W. Ferguson
7404 Aragon st Las Vegas, Nev. 89128
April 11, 1975
Las Vegas, Nevada

WITNESS
James W. Simmons
5572 Latigo st Las Vegas, Nevada 89119

WITNESS

Exhibit 1.12 Howard Hughes's Will: The Richard Robard version
Source: Howard Hughes, Will dated April 11, 1975, Will not probated.

Last Will and Testament

I Howard R. Hughes being of
sound and disposing mind and
memory, not acting under duress
fraud or the undue influence
of any person whomsoever
and being a resident of Las Vegas
Nevada declare that this
is to be my last Will
and revoke all other Wills
previously made by me —

After my death my estate
is to be divided as follows—

first one forth of all my assets to go to Hughes Med-
ical Institute of Miami —

second one eight of assets
to be deviled among
the University of Texas —
Rice Institute of Technology
of Houston —
the University of Nevada
and the University of Calif.
Howard R. Hu

Exhibit 1.13 Howard Hughes's Will: The Melvin DuMar (Dummar) version

Source: Howard Hughes, Will dated March 19, 1968, Will not probated.

third: one sixteenth to Church
of Jesus Christ of Latterday
Saints — David O. Makey Jr.

Forth: one sixteenth to establish a home for Orphan
Cildren —

Fifth: one sixteenth of assets
to go to Boy Scouts
of America:

sixth: one sixteenth; to be
divided among Jean Peters of
Los Angeles and Ella Rice
of Houston —

seventh: one sixteenth of assets
to William R. Lommis of
Houston, Texas —

eighth: one sixteenth to go
to Melvin Du Mar of
Gabbs Nevada —

devided amoung my
personal aids at the time
of my death -

tenth: one sixteenth to be
used as school scholarship
fund for entire Country -

The spruce goose is to be given
to the City of Long Beach, Cali.

The remainder of My
estate is to be devided among
the key men of the company
I own at the time of my
death.

I appoint Noah Dietrich
as the executer of this Will -

signed the 19 day of
March 1968

Howard R. Hughes

= page three =

Exhibit 1.13 (Continued)

and Howard. In that film, the late Jason Robards portrayed a rather scraggly looking Howard Hughes, who is picked up after a motorcycle accident by a trucker named Melvin Dummar. In gratitude for Mr. Dummar's kindness, Hughes allegedly wrote a Will bequeathing one sixteenth (1/16th) of his then estate, which would have been worth approximately $150million, to Melvin. Unfortunately for Melvin and the many worthy charities named in that purported Will, such as the Boy Scouts of America, after a lengthy trial about the validity of the purported Will, the court did not accept that one either.

With none of his purported Wills ever being accepted for probate, Hughes' estate's assets passed by *intestacy*, which means without a valid Will, so state law determined how the property would be distributed. After the payment of hundreds of millions of dollars of state and federal estate taxes, and accounting and legal fees, substantial assets were passed to Hughes' distant cousins, perhaps the most laughing of "laughing heirs." By failing to have most, if not all, of his estate pass to worthy charitable organizations such as his beloved Howard Hughes Medical Institute, Howard Hughes cost his estate a bundle in unnecessary estate taxes. In view of the magnitude of those taxes, Howard Hughes made a mega-mistake by not leaving a properly executed Last Will and Testament.

Mistake #8: **Dying Intestate, or Without a Will**

Having read a handful of estate planning mistakes, you may be wondering why it is so important to have a Will. After all, many of the celebrities discussed in the preceding chapters had Wills, yet many of them experienced execution problems.

Well, the answer is simple—not having an estate plan can result in significant additional expenses, taxes, and legal fees, not to mention the undue aggravation and agitation it may cause your family members, friends, or acquaintances. As such, estate planning mistake #8 is dying without a valid Will or alternative estate plan.

Without a Will, a Court may appoint an administrator to administer your estate, rather than your selecting an executor of your choice. The terms of your Will also determine how your property is to be distributed after your death instead of by each state's laws of intestacy.

For example, most states would provide that if a person dies without a Will or alternative estate plan in place, that his assets would pass in some statutorily specified proportion to his children and surviving spouse, if any. If the assets of the decedent are substantial, then the portion passing to the children and not qualifying for the marital deduction could result in significant and unnecessary state and federal estate taxes, all of which could have been avoided with a properly drafted Will. Ask the young widow whose 35-year-old husband died, leaving one son and a $20 million estate. Because he had no Will, under the laws of intestacy, approximately one-half, or $10 million passed to the son—a $5-million blunder. Even the simplest Will, leaving all the property outright or in trust to the surviving spouse, would have saved millions of dollars in estate taxes.

I recently handled an estate involving an 85-year-old Irish spinster who never married, whom we will call "Molly" for the purpose of this anecdote. Molly had been planning to sign a Will in which she left her million-dollar-plus estate to her favorite cousin, with whom she had a very close relationship, literally and figuratively, as he lived across the street from her. Unfortunately for her favorite cousin, Molly never did sign a Will, and she died intestate. That meant all of her 12 surviving cousins became her "distributees," or legal heirs, in accordance with New York State law. To add insult to injury, of the 12 legal heirs, 2 were on the decedent's paternal side and 10 were on the maternal side. That meant the two paternal cousins received approximately $250,000 each and the ten maternal cousins, including her closest cousin, each received around $50,000. That estate, which was handled by the Public Administrator, took an unusually long time to administer, because a kinship hearing was required to establish to the satisfaction of the Queens County Surrogate's Court who the legal heirs were. The decedent was of Irish heritage and many of her relatives still resided in Ireland, and the Court Referee and some of the attorneys needed to travel to Ireland to take the testimony of certain relatives. The expenses of that kinship hearing were borne by all of the beneficiaries.

The problems that arise as a result of the failure to properly attend to your estate planning are many, and it is a big mistake to put off planning for the inevitable—death and taxes.

Notes

1. Martin Luther King, Jr., Died Intestate, Fulton County Court of Ordinary, Fulton County, Atlanta, GA.
2. Robert F. Kennedy, Will dated December 17, 1953, proved June 13, 1968, File Number 4638-1968 Surrogate's Court, County of New York, New York, NY.
3. Ibid.
4. Ted Ammon, Will dated August 22, 2005, proved November 13, 2001, File Number 4105-2005, Surrogate's Court, County of New York, New York, NY.
5. Ray Charles, Will dated February 5, 1997, proved September 21, 2004, Case Number BP 087329, Superior Court of California, County of Los Angeles, Los Angeles, CA.

CHAPTER 2

Mistakes Involving Tangible Personal Property

Although the tangible personal property in an estate is often not of great monetary value, it often leads to strong personal conflict because of its great sentimental value. If it is property, such as a work of art, jewelry, or a pre-PETA fur coat, the problems are often even more severe due to the fact that unique tangible property is often not easily divisible.

It is surprising what people leave behind in their homes. I have stumbled upon guns, marijuana, cocaine, pornography, and even some dirty laundry in some of the estates that we have handled.

In the twenty-first century, the family pet is often the most sensitive type of tangible personal property; pets require special practical and legal attention. But when it comes to providing for pets, Leona Helmsley showed us how a person might go too far; she provided for her pooch, Trouble (but not two of her grandchildren) from her vast estate after she was gone.

Mistake #9: Nemo Dat Quo Non Habet (Latin for "He Who Has Not Cannot Give")

In my first year of law school, I had a Professor named William Schwartz who was one of the best teachers I ever had. He taught us so many important concepts of property law in an unforgettable manner. One of his favorite and often repeated Latin phrases was "nemo dat quo non habet," which is translated loosely as "You can't give what you don't have." That is especially important when it comes time to sign your Will.

It is always possible that a testator might view his or her Will as a work of fiction, in which he generously bequeaths Rembrandt paintings, diamond rings, or other objects of great or little value that he does not in fact own. Alternatively, the person owns the items at the time that the Will is signed but sells, loses, or gives them away by the time he or she dies. Another possibility is that the person still owns the items specified in his Will when he dies, but because his debts exceed his assets, his estate's creditors have priority in terms of being paid by the estate ahead of the beneficiaries named in the Will of a bequest of a particular item of tangible personal property. The tangible property remaining in an insolvent estate might have to be sold to satisfy the creditors' liens.

This issue reminds me of the Will of the one and only Sammy Davis, Jr., whose career as a singer, dancer, and actor began at age three and spanned more than 60 years until his death at age 64 in 1990. Davis was as notorious for his lifestyle as part of Hollywood's Rat Pack in the 1950s and 1960s as he was for his success as a star of stage, screen, and song. Unfortunately, the "Candy Man" also battled cocaine and alcohol addiction throughout his life.

The often-bejeweled Mr. Bojangles made certain in his Will, which was executed approximately two months before his death, that several of his friends would have a little token of his "Samminess" to remember him by. For example, Davis made the following bequests of jewelry to his friends:[1]

- I give to my dear friend FORTUNATUS RICARD, my pinky ring
- I give to my dear friend JOHN R. CLIMACO my brown diamond ring
- I give to my dear friend SHIRLEY RHODES the sum of Twenty-Five Thousand Dollars ($25,000.00) to be used as "fun money," along with my large diamond ring

Although he was not known for his affinity for firearms, Mr. Davis made three specific bequests of guns in his Will:

- I give to my friend CLINT EASTWOOD my "Gary Cooper" gun
- I give to the GENE AUTRY WESTERN MUSEUM all remaining pieces of my Western gun collection
- I give to my dear friend BRIAN DELLOW my personal Chrysler automobile and my non-Western gun collection

Finally, Mr. Davis made certain to provide for his wife and children with regard to his "items of sentimentality."

- "I give to my beloved wife, ALTOVISE, and my beloved children the right to select and divide amongst themselves, for their ownership, my papers, memorabilia, musical arrangements, photographs, awards and other items of sentimentality. Those not selected by my wife or any of my children shall be directed one half (½) to WILBERFORCE COLLEGE in Ohio and one half (½) to HOWARD UNIVERSITY in Washington D.C., equally . . . "

Unfortunately, it is unclear whether any of the people named received anything pursuant to these bequests, as Sammy reportedly was bankrupt at the time of his death and owed around $6 million in debts, far in excess of the fair market value of his assets when he died.

It is a mistake to bequeath in your Will specific tangible personal property that you do not own, or that you may not own when you die, because it creates false expectations for the named recipient and could lead to aggravation, hurt feelings, and unnecessary additional estate administration expenses.

Mistake #10: Not Properly Documenting the Delivery and Completion of a Gift

You have finally done it. You have convinced your mother-in-law to give you that diamond ring or Tiffany silver bowl of hers that you have always coveted. She says that she is giving it to you, but the problem is that she just never actually gives it to you. A *gift* may be defined as a voluntary, gratuitous transfer of property from one person to another without any *consideration* (i.e., payment). The four essential legal requirements for the gift to be valid and effective are:

1. The intent of the donor
2. The requisite mental capacity of the donor
3. Completed delivery of the gift
4. Acceptance of the gift by the donee, or recipient, of the gift

If you can get past numbers 1 and 2, then you need to be sure that you have addressed numbers 3 and 4, with which a donee has some ability to offer some assistance. The simplest way to avoid a problem is to physically take possession of the item, and add it to your own insurance policy as soon as possible. You should also ask your mother-in-law to take the item off of the rider to her insurance policy and to sign a Deed of Gift.

You may be asking yourself, "What is a Deed of Gift?"

A Deed of Gift is a written instrument that is signed and delivered by the donor of the gift to the donee of the gift; because it is a gift, there is no consideration for the donation.

The Deed of Gift consists of an accurate description of the property being gifted and should include the name and address of the person who is to receive the gift. It should be signed and dated by the person giving the gift at the end of the document. It can be witnessed, notarized, sworn to, or whatever other bell or whistle you would like. It can be signed in duplicate, and the donee of the gift would be well advised to keep an original of the signed document in a safe, secure place. It is a simple written document that can have a powerful impact and help promptly resolve any questions related to the facts of the gift. It can also have a negative impact, if the signed original document cannot be located if, and when, the validity of the alleged gift is being questioned.

Thus, if you are the happy recipient of a gift from someone, and you believe that there might be a challenge to that gift sometime in the future, don't look at that gift in the face until you have arranged for a Deed of Gift to be signed by the giver of the gift to you. Finally, take possession of the property as soon as possible, because as the adage goes, possession is nine-tenths of the law. It is a mistake not to take care of the paperwork in connection with the gift.

Unfortunately, depending on the value of the gift, the paperwork might also include gift tax returns that need to be filed with our friends at the Internal Revenue Service.

It is a mistake to fail to properly document any lifetime gifts that you might be making or receiving.

Mistake #11: Selling Valuable Tangible Personal Property Too Close to Death

Speaking of the Internal Revenue Service, the estate of Jacqueline Kennedy Onassis, who died at the age of 64 in 1994, reportedly had some protracted discussions with the IRS related to the true fair market value of the tangible personal property in her estate, which the estate had valued at $6 million, but which the IRS thought was closer to $35 million.

The lengthy and sophisticated Will of Jacqueline Kennedy Onassis, known to the world as Jackie O, reveals what a sensitive, generous, and thoughtful person she was. Jackie's Will, which was signed less than two months before she died, includes numerous detailed bequests, such as the following gifts of tangible personal property to certain people who were obviously important to her:

A. ". . . to my friend, MAURICE TEMPELSMAN . . . my Greek alabaster head of a woman . . . "
B. ". . . to my friend, RACHEL (BUNNY) L. MELLON, in appreciation of her designing the Rose Garden in the White House . . . my
   - "Indian miniature 'Lovers watching rain clouds,' Kangra, about 1780 . . . and my large Indian miniature with giltwood frame
   - "'Gardens of the Palace of the Rajh,' a panoramic view of a pink walled garden blooming with orange flowers, with the Rajh being entertained in a pavilion by musicians and dancers . . .
C. ". . . to my friend [attorney and co-executor] ALEXANDER D. FORGER . . . my copy of John F. Kennedy's Inaugural Address signed by Robert Frost . . . "[2]

After those very specific bequests, which all needed to be valued as part of her estate, Jackie provided that the balance of her tangible personal property, including "my collection of letters, papers, and documents, my personal effects, my furniture, furnishings, rugs, pictures, books, silver, plate, linen, china, glassware, objects of art, wearing apparel, jewelry, automobiles and their accessories, and all other household goods owned by me . . . " (including the kitchen sink) were to pass in equal shares to her two children, Caroline and John.[3]

It is noteworthy that Jackie's Will also contained a legal mechanism whereby the children could renounce and disclaim their respective interests in the tangible property within nine months of their mother's death. Any property so disclaimed by the children would have then passed as follows:

1. " . . . such items . . . which relate to the life and work of my late husband, John F. Kennedy, to JOHN FITZGERALD KENNEDY LIBRARY INCORPORATED, Boston, Massachusetts . . . "
2. " . . . the balance of said tangible personal property shall be sold and the net proceeds of sale shall be added to my residuary estate . . . "[4]

Tangible personal property obviously meant a lot to Jackie O, and it was also worth a lot in her estate, and the IRS noticed. One way to prove "fair market value" of tangible personal property for estate tax purposes to the satisfaction of the IRS is to sell an item at a public auction, where there are many willing buyers under no compulsion to buy. Caroline and John chose not to renounce the vast bulk of the tangible personal property bequeathed to them, and it was that property, sold at a memorable auction at Sotheby's, that grossed close to $35 million for Caroline and John. The view of the IRS was that those sale prices represented fair market value for estate tax purposes, and therefore the IRS expected to levy an estate tax rate of 55 percent on the value of that property. The estate, on the other hand, had submitted a date of death appraisal with the estate tax return that reflected the appraised fair market values, which were much lower than the actual sale prices. In view of the substantial differential between a capital gains rate of 28 percent, which would have been applicable if the property were valued for estate tax purposes at its appraised value, and the estate tax rate of 55 percent, and that there were tens of millions of dollars involved, the potential tax savings would be huge, and worth fighting about.

It has been reported that the estate reached a compromise settlement with the IRS that is not a matter of public record. However, if Caroline and John had just waited to sell these valuable items until *after* the conclusion of the IRS estate tax return examination, the question of an alternative actual sale price value would not have come up. It may have been a mistake to sell all of Jackie O's fabulous jewelry, clothing, and even mundane bric-a-brac at a public auction too soon. It is not likely that the Kennedy/Onassis luster and value would have been diminished by waiting another year or two so that the coast would be clear of any pirates waving the flag of the IRS.

Mistake 12: Bequeathing Tangible Personal Property That You Do Not Own

No doubt, Jackie O had a great amount of very valuable "stuff." Many people just have a large amount of stuff that is of not great value, especially when you try to sell it. The IRS and/or state tax authorities have not been overly focused on valuing the stuff that most people own when they die. The taxing authorities will often accept a nominal valuation of the *tangible personal property* on the estate tax return, if an estate tax return is even required.

However, sometimes a decedent's Last Will and Testament attracts the scrutiny of the taxing authorities if it includes a bequest of an extensive list of types of tangible personal property such as " . . . my boats, airplanes, cars, silverware, paintings, sculptures, drawings, etchings, photographs, china, linen, jewelry, gold bullion, bric-a-brac, L.P. records, cassettes, compact discs, computer equipment, garden tools . . . " I have not yet seen a Will that specifically bequeaths the kitchen sink, but it will come. I have seen many Wills over the years that include a detailed list of different types of tangible personal property, including some that the testator does not even own.

In his Will, Yankee baseball legend Joe DiMaggio bequeathed all his " . . . household furnishings, silverware, china or linens, automobiles and jewelry . . . " to one of his two granddaughters, Paula Sue DiMaggio.[5] Do we really believe that the Yankee Clipper who had been married to Marilyn Monroe cared much about his "china and linens" as much as his lawyer did?

Once, during an estate tax examination of an estate with a Will that was not prepared by me, the IRS agent needed to be satisfied that the decedent did not own a boat, as mentioned in his Will.

We provided an affidavit to the effect that any such boat was no longer afloat among the decedent's assets, and the agent accepted our representations.

It is a mistake to provide too much detail and mention specific types of tangible personal property in your Will, especially if you do not even own that type of property. Unless there is a good reason to mention specific items of tangible personal property in a Will, it is usually better to keep it simple by bequeathing "all of my tangible personal property" to my spouse, children, executor, or whomever else you want to have it or arrange for its distribution. Exactly what that property is will be determined and ascertained as of the date of death, and will not be pursuant to a document that may have been prepared many years before death and includes specific items of tangible personal property that the testator never even owned.

Mistake #13: Mentioning Too Many Details in Your Will

For many reasons, in recent years, Wills have become less detailed when it comes to the disposition of the tangible personal property that the decedent owned. But in decades past, it was not uncommon for a person to make meticulous provisions regarding the disposition of his favorite material things. Take W.C. Fields, for example.

William C. Fields, also known as W.C. Fields and as Bill Fields, signed his Last Will and Testament in 1943, about three years before he died of cirrhosis of the liver (among other maladies) in a sanitarium in Pasadena, California on Christmas Day in 1946. On the same day that he signed his Will, W.C. Fields also signed the following detailed letter of instructions to his Executor, Magda Michael, regarding the disposition of his tangible personal property. As you can see from that letter, which is reproduced in full in Exhibit 2.1, Fields was very exact in describing the various items of tangible personal property that he owned, including his liquor collection, which he divided into three equal shares and bequeathed to three of his favorite drinking buddies.

Although the list of items bequeathed by W.C. Fields provides a fascinating glimpse into the life and liquor cabinet of one of the greatest American comedians, it seems like it might just be too much information to be made public. Do we really need, or want, to know that Fields left his "shoes, underwear, shirts, one third of my liquor . . . " to his brother Walter Fields? Or that his friend Adele Vallery Clines was the beneficiary of "2 fly catchers"?

To my Executor, Magda Michael:

In subparagraph 16 of the Third Paragraph of my last will

and testament, executed today, I bequeath to you in trust

the following articles of furniture and personal effects,

for delivery to the following persons:

To Charles Beyer: My desk, chair, chest, waste basket,
desk, knick-knacks, side table for
telephone, one open book case, revolving
book case, two wood baskets by fireplace,
Executone set, large steel cabinet and
contents, camera (he gave me) one-third
liquor, golf bag and clubs, one-third
ties, square trunk in basement contain-
ing books of press notices and programs,
also all the books of press notices and
programs upstairs, garden furniture,
station wagon, decanter set, 3 birdcage
stands, 2 ladders, ice chest, champagne
bucket.

To Carlotta Monti: One typewriter, red Taylor Trunk, large
Webster's Unabridged Dictionary, my small
dictionary and Roget's Thesaurus, Packard
Bell radio, with recording equipment,
one open book case, Encyclopedia Brit-
tanica, electric clock, secret filing
cabinet ("Secretaire") rubber mattress,
picture of me in Honolulu, one set of
gold dishes in closet, one set of gold
lamps in closet, blue Angora knit robe,
smaller steel cabinet in office, secretary's desk and chair, two bottles Shalimar
in closet, large pair field glasses (Zephyr
7x35) share silverware in trunk and kitchen-
ware with Adele Clines, Frigidaire, water
softener, fireless cooker, 1 croquet set,
1 umbrella, records, 1 foot heater, electric
steam table, large safe, rubbing table, also
my 16-cylinder Cadillac limousine.

-1-

Exhibit 2.1 List of tangible personal property owned by W.C. Fields

Source: W.C. Fields, Will dated April 28, 1943, proved December 31, 1946, Case Number 264050, Superior Court of California, County of Los Angeles, Los Angeles, CA.

To Brother Walter Fields: General Electric portable radio, traveling clock, one-half remaining trunks in basement, one-third neckties (first choice) all of my clothes, shoes, underwear, shirts, one third of my liquor, one rubbing table, 2 car trunks, 2 auto robes, billiard table & chairs, ping pong table.

To Sister Adel Smith: Waterbury ships clock, one-half of the remaining trunks in basement, 2 bottles of Shalimar.

To Magda Michael: One typewriter, large dictaphone, 1 croquet set, 1 umbrella, 1 food heater.

To Gregory LaCava: revolvers, one third liquor, large electric fan, pictures taken in Soboba, one set of gold dishes in closet, one set gold lamps in closet, electric refrigerator on wheels.

To Adele Vallery Clines: All the glasses upstairs and down, washing machine (Bendix) silverware in trunk and kitchen ware (share with Carlotta Monti) bottle of Shalimar, square glass ash tray, ash stands, 2 fly catchers, adjustable square tables in office.

To Bob Murphy: Pictures in rubbing room, 1/2 Decker pictures

To Hershal Crockett: Double pen set on my desk and brown pencil to match.

To Frank Clines: Paint spray gun and equipment, all paints, big jack, carpenter tools, etc.

To Gene Fowler: Howard heating cabinet, all my pens and pencils except those before mentioned, also my small dictaphone, small leather trunk and contents.

To Dave Chasen: 1/2 Decker pictures.

To Bob Howard: 2 wooden chairs in office, rocking chair, bar chairs and fixtures.

To all my friends, herein mentioned: Distribute the wooden paper holders I had made.

To George Moran: My jewelry, cuff links, tie clips and chains.

If lease of house cannot be broken, my brother Walter, or sister Adel Smith or Carlotta Monti or Magda Michael may occupy it until end of first year.

Dated this 28 day
of April, 1943.

W. C. Fields

Exhibit 2.1 *(Continued)*

Mistakes Involving Tangible Personal Property

Besides the economic benefit of deemphasizing tangible personal property for estate tax purposes, it might be a mistake to provide too much information about your tangible personal property. Suppose Fields had promised those two fly swatters to somebody else. Not only might that person's feelings be hurt, but she might have felt like a sucker who couldn't get a break, which would probably have suited the freewheeling and eccentric W.C. Fields just fine.

Mistake #14: Not Including Any Details in Your Will

Now let's go from the overly detailed Will of W.C. Fields to the other extreme. It could be a big mistake to make no provisions whatsoever for the disposition of your tangible personal property, especially if your name is Andy Warhol and you died in 1987 with an estate then worth more than $500 million.

A large portion of Warhol's wealth consisted of lots and lots of "stuff," including multiple houses and warehouses full of extraordinarily valuable artworks created by the one and only Andy Warhol himself. Warhol's stuff also included extensive and exceptional collections of cookie jars, Fiesta dinnerware, cigar-store Indians, watches, funeral urns, toys, jewelry, furniture, personal effects, probably a Campbell's soup can or two, and much more. Like Picasso, Andy Warhol was an artist who achieved such exceptional fame during his lifetime that everything he touched became extraordinarily valuable.

Despite the extensive property owned and collected by Andy Warhol, there were no provisions for any of it in Andy Warhol's 1982 Will, which was prepared by one of New York's finest law firms. After making relatively small bequests to his two surviving brothers and to his friend and executor, Fred Hughes, Warhol left his entire estate to a nebulous foundation, The Foundation for Visual Arts, that had not even been created at the time of his death.

Exhibit 2.2 shows the excerpt from Andy Warhol's Last Will and Testament that directs the formation of The Foundation for Visual Arts and gives Warhol's vast residuary estate to that as-of-then unformed Foundation.

Warhol's estate plan may have been proper and sound from an estate tax point of view, because there would have been little or no estate taxes payable in view of the unlimited charitable deduction that would apply, but one would have liked to have had the artist's input into how and where he wanted his collections disbursed. One of the things that the Foundation has done is to establish a museum in Pittsburgh, Pennsylvania—a city that Andy Warhol had seemed to want to leave behind. Once he made the scene in New York City, he did not look back. It may have been a mistake for Andy Warhol not to be more focused, by his attorneys or others, on what would and should happen to all of his stuff at the time of his inevitable demise.

FOURTH:

A. I DIRECT my Executor, within three months after his qualification, to incorporate or cause to be incorporated, a corporation in accordance with and under the provisions of the New York Not-For-Profit Corporation Law, or any similar law of New York or any other State. Such corporation shall be a foundation for the advancement of the visual arts and shall be incorporated under the name of "THE FOUNDATION FOR VISUAL ARTS", or of similar name (here-inafter, the "foundation"). The certificate of incorporation of the foundation shall contain any and all provisions necessary to create a corporation bequests to which are deductible for United States estate tax purposes under section 2055 of the Internal Revenue Code of 1954, as amended from time to time before my death. Without limiting the generality of the foregoing, the certificate of incorporation (or other documents relating to the incorporation of the foundation) shall specifically state that the foundation is organized and operated exclusively for charitable purposes; no part

Exhibit 2.2 Excerpt from the Will of Andy Warhol

Source: Andy Warhol, Will dated March 11, 1982, File Number 1987-0824, Surrogate's Court, County of New York, New York, NY.

of its net earnings shall inure to the benefit of any private stockholder or individual; no part of its activities shall consist of carrying on propaganda, or otherwise attempting, to influence legislation; it shall not participate in, or intervene in (including the publishing or distributing of statements), any political campaign on behalf of any candidate for public office; and its directors shall be prohibited from engaging in any act (including, without limitation, the acts set forth in Section 406 of the New York Not-For-Profit Corporation Law, or any similar provision of the law of any other State) that would prevent any bequest to the foundation from qualifying as a deduction for my estate under section 2055 of the Internal Revenue Code, as amended.

B. I DIRECT that the following individuals shall be named as the initial Directors and corporate members of the foundation created pursuant to Section A of this Article: FREDERICK HUGHES, VINCENT FREEMONT and JOHN WARHOL.

Each of the individuals named herein shall have the right to refuse to serve as a Director and/or corporate member, and each Director and/or corporate member shall have the right to resign as a Director and/or corporate member, by an instrument delivered to the then acting Director or Directors and/or corporate member or members of the foundation. There shall always be three (3) Directors of the foundation; and if from time to time any Director named herein fails, refuses or ceases to act as a Director so that there are less than three (3) Directors of the foundation, the then acting corporate member or members (or, if there are none, my Executor) is or are authorized and empowered to name one or more substitute Directors so that there will always be three (3)

Exhibit 2.2 (*Continued*)

Mistakes Involving Tangible Personal Property

Directors of the foundation.

FIFTH:

I GIVE the balance of my residuary estate (after satisfaction of the bequests, if any, in Article THIRD hereof) to the
foundation created pursuant to Article FOURTH of this Will or if,
for any reason, such foundation shall not be incorporated or the
bequest herein shall not be deductible for United States estate ta:
purposes under Section 2055 of the Internal Revenue Code of 1954,
I do not GIVE such balance of my residuary estate to such foundation but, instead, I GIVE such balance of my residuary estate to
such one or more corporations, associations and organizations
for the advancement of the visual arts, bequests to which are
deductible under Section 2055 of the Internal Revenue Code of 1954,
and in such proportions as my Executor, in his discretion, shall
determine.

Mistake #15: Not Providing Properly for the Care of Your Pets After Your Death

Although domesticated pets and other animals in the twenty-first century have gained greater legal rights under various federal and state laws, for the purposes of estate law, a pet or other animal is still considered a form of *chattel*, and would be subsumed in the broad category of tangible personal property often used in Wills.

However, because pets are living creatures that can feel hunger, thirst, and pain, it is certainly more humane to provide for their ongoing care after the death of their human caretakers. It could be a life and death mistake, for your pet, if your Will or other planning documents are silent about what will happen to your pet or pets when you are gone. Those arrangements can be made through your Will, or through the terms of a trust that you establish during your lifetime.

Up-to-date estate planning documents are important but often do not become effective until someone has legal authority to act for your estate. As a result, there could be a dangerous and lonely interlude for your pet. On a practical level, it may be wise and prudent to provide for your pet by making lifetime arrangements with a relative, friend, or other caretaker, who has ongoing access to your home (i.e., a key) and authority to enter for the purposes of rescuing or taking care of your pet cat or pit bull.

Many of our clients feel strongly about providing for the future needs of their pets, who are increasingly considered important members of the family. The legal options may include a simple cash bequest, together with any pet or pets you may own at death, to someone who will take care of your pet without any strings attached. Alternatively, a client can establish a trust that will provide income and/or principal to take care of the pet for the rest of its life. Such a trust would require a trustee to administer it, and would also provide for what would happen to the funds remaining in the trust upon the death of Fido.

I have acted as the trustee of a $200,000 trust for the benefit of a cat named Ming (a real cat, not some dude who hangs out in jazz clubs), that had been owned by my deceased client, who had no other surviving family members. I made sure that all of Ming's pet food and other expenses were covered during his lifetime. Upon Ming's death, the funds remaining in the trust were to be given to Ming's caretaker, who had been the doorman in my late client's building. When Ming did die, at close to ten years of age, I had to make sure that Ming had not died as a result of foul play by her caretaker so that I could deliver the remaining funds to that caretaker. I arranged for an autopsy by an independent veterinarian, who confirmed that Ming had indeed died of natural causes. With the autopsy in hand, I could happily and responsibly deliver the substantial funds remaining in the trust to that doorman, whose young family could definitely use the money.

It is increasingly common to have our clients ask us about what they can do to protect their pets after their own demise. And there are many responsible and humanitarian options available to those who are concerned about the future of their beloved pets. But there may be certain people who take providing for their pets to the extreme, which reminds me of Leona Helmsley. The so-called Queen of Mean was anything but that to her pet dog, Trouble, either during her lifetime or after she went to stand guard in the great hotel lobby in the sky.

Mistake #16: Leaving Too Much Money for Your Pets After Your Death

Although the protection of the rights of pets and other animals represents a strong legal trend in the twenty-first century, in some cases, the financial needs of a pet can be provided for too generously.

Leona Helmsley provided for a $12 million trust for the benefit of her Maltese breed dog Trouble. With that kind of money, a person, or dog, could definitely get into a lot of trouble.

The page from Helmsley's 2007 Will that mentions the bequest for Trouble, which was bequeathed to an *inter vivos* trust established in 2005, is reproduced in Exhibit 2.3.

The terms of the July 2005 trust are not a matter of public record, but it appears that dog Trouble is the sole beneficiary of that trust for the rest of her life. We must bear in mind that Trouble was accustomed to a very high standard of living, as she spent a great deal of time in Leona's lap of luxury.

So how is poor Trouble doing with her $12 million trust fund? Trouble got a $10 million haircut. Shortly after their appointment, the executors of Leona Helmsley's Will filed a petition with the Surrogate's Court pursuant to New York's Estates, Powers and Trusts Law to reduce, from $12 million to $2 million, the amount to be transferred to the trustees of the trust for the benefit of Trouble. The Court approved the proposed reduction in the amount of Trouble's trust fund. The pampered pooch will have to find a way to survive on a paltry $2 million for the remainder of her lifetime.[6] Apparently, there has already been an impact on Trouble's lifestyle, as she has recently relocated to Florida, perhaps attempting to avoid the high cost of living in New York City.

(3) If my brother ALVIN ROSENTHAL survives me, I leave the sum of Ten Million Dollars ($10,000,000) to the trust established for his benefit under paragraph B of Article FOUR.

E.   I direct that the following bequests be made for each of the following persons, outright and not in trust:

(1) If my brother ALVIN ROSENTHAL survives me, I leave the sum of Five Million Dollars ($5,000,000) to him.

(2) If my grandson DAVID PANZIRER survives me, I leave the sum of Five Million Dollars ($5,000,000) to him.

(3) If my grandson WALTER PANZIRER survives me, I leave the sum of Five Million Dollars ($5,000,000) to him.

(4) If my chauffeur NICHOLAS CELEA survives me and at the time of my death is employed by me or any Helmsley entity, I leave the sum of One Hundred Thousand Dollars ($100,000) to him.

F.   I leave the sum of Twelve Million Dollars ($12,000,000) to the Trustees of the LEONA HELMSLEY JULY 2005 TRUST, established under an instrument dated on or about the date of this Will, to be disposed of in accordance with the provisions of that Trust agreement. I leave my dog, Trouble, if she survives me, to my brother, ALVIN ROSENTHAL, if he survives me, or if he does not survive me, to my grandson DAVID PANZIRER. I direct that when my dog, Trouble, dies, her remains shall be buried next to my remains in the Helmsley Mausoleum at Woodlawn Cemetery, Bronx, New York, or in such other mausoleum as I may be interred pursuant to this will.

G.   I have not made any provisions in this Will for my grandson CRAIG PANZIRER or my granddaughter MEEGAN PANZIRER for reasons which are known to them.

ARTICLE TWO
TAXES AND EXPENSES

All of my funeral expenses, last illness expenses, and estate administration expenses shall be paid from my residuary estate. All estate and inheritance taxes (including interest and penalties thereon but not including any generation-skipping transfer taxes imposed under Chapter 13 of the Internal Revenue Code of 1986, as amended (the "Code")) on all assets passing under this Will shall be charged against my residuary estate.

3

Exhibit 2.3 Excerpt from the Will of Leona Helmsley

Source: Leona Helmsley, Will dated July 15, 2005, proved March 21, 2008, File Number 2968-2007, Surrogate's Court, County of New York, New York, NY.

Mistake #17: Giving the Same Tangible Personal Property Item to More Than One Person

If you feel that you must bequeath particular items of tangible property in your Will to certain people, be careful—and make sure that the attorney preparing your Will is even more careful. Be sure that the item of chattel being bequeathed is carefully described so that there can be no confusion about the exact item you meant.

For instance, do not bequeath your "engagement ring," especially if you have been engaged more than once. Instead, carefully describe the setting and diamond of the ring, including the number of carats, color, clarity, and any other c-word that you like. Beside jewelry, fur coats, cars, and various types of ultimately fungible property require great specificity so that there will not be a cat fight over which particular item was intended by the testator.

I have seen Wills in which the exact same item of property was bequeathed to two or more people. This error is often the result of a typographical or drafting error (or sheer stupidity), and can also lead to unnecessary expense and aggravation for those involved.

In summary, it is a big mistake to bequeath specific items of tangible personal property in your Will if you are not crystal clear in describing the items you have in mind. If there is any confusion about those items after your demise, the executor of your Will may need to spend unnecessary time and estate money to resolve the problem, whether by litigation, negotiation, mediation, arbitration . . . or cat fight.

Mistake #18: Not Properly Providing for the Disposition of Your Artworks After Your Death

If you are an über-famous artist such as Andy Warhol, it is definitely a good idea to consider where you would like at least a few of your most important works of art to reside after your demise. Andy Warhol died at the relatively young age of 58 in 1987, and based on the multimillion dollar prices that are being paid for his artworks more than 20 years later, it seems clear that Warhol and his art will never be forgotten. Another important twentieth-century artist who was also represented by art dealer Leo Castelli, was my friend Roy Lichtenstein.

I had the pleasure and great honor of assisting Roy Lichtenstein and his muse/wife, Dorothy, with their estate planning. The Last Will and Testament of Roy Lichtenstein, made in 1991, is a matter of public record, having been offered and accepted for probate by the Suffolk County Surrogate's Court of the State of New York. It would not be appropriate for me to divulge any confidential discussions that I had with Roy and Dorothy, but because Roy's Will is a matter of public record, I have no problem reproducing the provisions of that Will that pertain to the disposition of a few of Roy's greatest masterpieces to three favored museums and numerous other artworks to various friends and relatives (see Exhibit 2.4). Suffice it to say that not only was a charitable bequest a smart thing to do for estate tax purposes, but now the public will always have access to these priceless masterpieces by one of the great artists of the twentieth century.

Unfortunately, a minuscule percentage of working artists achieve the fame of Roy Lichtenstein or Andy Warhol. Most artists toil at their craft in relative obscurity and pass away with numerous works of art crammed into their homes or studios. Oftentimes, those artworks

OF

ROY LICHTENSTEIN

I, ROY LICHTENSTEIN, domiciled in the Village of Southampton in the Town of Southampton in the County of Suffolk in the State of New York, and a citizen of the United States of America, make, publish and declare this as and to be my Last Will and Testament, hereby revoking any and all of my prior Wills and Codicils.

FIRST: <u>Directions to Executors</u>

A. I direct my Executors to pay my final medical bills, funeral related costs and all other estate administration expenses, as tax deductible expenses of the administration of my estate.

B. I direct my Executors to pay as tax deductible expenses of the administration of my estate, all expenses related to the tangible personal property bequeathed herein, including insuring, securing, storing, restoring, packing, mailing, delivering, dealers', auctioneers', or other sellers' commissions, costs or fees, and all other similar expenses.

C. I direct my Executors to sell such of my Artistic Property (as hereinafter defined) as they, in their sole discretion, determine necessary to pay taxes and to effect distribution of my estate.

SECOND: <u>Bequests of Specific Works of Art</u>

I give and bequeath all my right, title and interest, including all my copyright interest therein, in the following works of art created by me, to such of the charitable institutions and persons named below as shall survive me:

      A. To the MUSEUM OF MODERN ART located in New York, New York, my painting entitled "Bauhaus Stairway" (1988).

      B. To the NATIONAL GALLERY OF ART located in Washington, D.C., my painting entitled "Look Mickey" (1961).

      C. To the SOLOMON R. GUGGENHEIM MUSEUM located in New

Exhibit 2.4 Excerpt from the Will of Roy Lichtenstein

Source: Roy Lichtenstein, Will dated December 3, 1992, proved October 19, 1997, Surrogate's Court, County of Suffolk, Riverhead, NY.

York, New York, my painting entitled "Grrrrrrr!"
(1965)(IN).

D. To my sister, RENEE TOLCOTT, my painting entitled
"Sunset" (1964)(RL Catalogue # 1078) and my Aubusson
Tapestry (RL Catalogue #1011)(currently located in the
Bernardi apartment).

E. To my niece, LYNN TOLCOTT, my painting entitled
"Untitled Reflection" (1989) (RL Catalogue # 1170;
LC Catalogue # 1089).

F. To my nephew, MICHAEL TOLCOTT, my painting entitled
"Untitled Reflection" (1989)(RL Catalogue # 1166;
LC Catalogue # 1091).

G. To my friends, PAUL WALDMAN and DIANE WALDMAN, or the
survivor of them, my painting entitled "Bluefish"
(1973).

H. To my friend, FREDERIC TUTEN, my painting
entitled "Mirror" (1970)(LC Catalogue # 572).

I. To my friend, KENNETH GOLDGLIT, my painting entitled
"Abstraction with Guitar" (1975)(LC Catalogue # 705).

J. To my friend, CASSANDRA LOZANO, the patinated bronze
"Profile Head V" (1988)(2/6)(RL Catalogue # 0033; LC
Catalogue # 1073).

K. To my friend, JAMES DEPASQUALE, the patinated bronze
"Mobile III" (1990)(6/6)(RL Catalogue # 0048).

L. To my friend, ROBERT MCKEEVER, the patinated bronze
"Galetea" (1990)(6/6)(RL Catalogue # 1027)

have no place to go; maybe a few end up on a friend's or, better yet, on a museum's wall. An artist's works of art often feel like children to him. It is so important that the artist die knowing that he has provided for the future of his children, and that requires planning.

This is a big problem for many artists. Lucky for them, there are solutions to this problem; financially successful artists can establish charitable foundations, but all artists can arrange for their artworks to be protected and preserved by caring friends and relatives. If you are an artist, it is a mistake not to discuss what will happen to your artworks after your death with your family, friends, museum curators, collectors, and, of course, with the attorney who is preparing your Will and assisting with your estate planning.

Mistake #19: Not Providing for Your Tangible Personal Property in a Revocable Living Trust

Although many attorneys across America tout the benefits of using a revocable living trust as the primary estate planning document instead of a Will, it is not uncommon for those same attorneys to fail to provide for the disposition of tangible personal property pursuant to the terms of the trust that is established. I have seen this mistake made even by experienced legal counsel.

Although your attorney may believe that he has transferred all of your assets into the name of your revocable living trust while you are alive, he may have forgotten about your tangible personal property.

If your tangible property is not expressly transferred into the name of your trust through the listing of the tangible personal property on a schedule attached to the trust agreement, or by a subsequent instrument of transfer, then the property may still be owned by you on the day that you die. If that property has more than financial or sentimental value, then it may end up thwarting your best-laid plans. As a result, it may *not* avoid probate and have to pass by your Will, since it was never successfully transferred into your trust.

It is an oversight and a mistake not to arrange for your tangible personal property to be transferred into the name of your lifetime trust during your lifetime.

Notes

1. Sammy Davis, Jr., Will dated March 12, 1990, Case Number BP 002045, Superior Court of California, County of Los Angeles, Los Angeles, CA.
2. Jaqueline Kennedy Onassis, Will dated May 15, 1984, proved October 25, 1984, File Number 3100-1985, Surrogate's Court, County of New York, New York, NY.

3. Ibid.
4. Ibid.
5. Joe DiMaggio, Will dated May 21, 1996, proved March 3, 1999, Case Number PRC 990001496, Circuit Court, Broward County, Ft. Lauderdale, FL.
6. Leona Helmsley, Will dated July 15, 2005, proved March 21, 2008, File Number 2968-2007, Surrogate's Court, County of New York, New York, NY.

Mistakes Involving Real Estate

Because everyone has to live somewhere, almost every estate—large or small—includes rental or ownership of real property, or some similar ownership interest, such as owning stock in a cooperative corporation (which is quite common in New York City). Property ownership raises all kinds of issues and often leads to all kinds of mistakes. The practical problems described in the following pages provide a helpful road map for the unwary by highlighting the potential traps and pitfalls, including water pipes that may burst in the winter.

Mistake #20: Not Confirming How Title Is Held to Real Estate Before or Right After Death

When it comes to books and business, titles may or may not be important, but when it comes to real estate, title is critical. If a house or other real property is owned by two people as *joint tenants with a right of survivorship* (jtwros), then upon the death of one of them, the ownership passes to the other by operation of law, and not pursuant to a Last Will and Testament. If the property is owned in one individual's name or as a "tenant in common," and not as a jtwros, then the property will pass pursuant to the Will of the decedent or in accordance with the laws of intestacy.

If an estate plan has been structured upon the erroneous belief that a piece of property is owned in the wife's name individually, but it is in fact owned by her as a jtwros with her husband, then an estate plan can be undermined and ineffectual. Unfortunately, this mistake occurred in the estate of my wife's mother, who had been represented by one of New York's most well-known trusts and estates attorneys, who practiced at one of New York's largest and most prominent law firms. (It may have been a bigger mistake for her not to consult with, or retain the services of, her son-in-law, who was also a well-known trusts and estates attorney, but that mistake is another story.)

The Will of my mother-in-law included provisions for a so-called bypass or credit shelter trust, which was designed to protect the allowable federal exemption amount, then $1 million, from the imposition of estate tax in the surviving spouse's estate. However, because the attorney erroneously thought that she owned a small building in Manhattan in her name individually, but in fact owned it as a jtwros with her husband, it passed automatically to him upon her death, and was not available as an asset to fund the credit shelter trust under her Will. Because she did not use it (i.e., the tax-exempt amount), she lost it, and lost the potential tax savings that might have resulted if the plan had worked. As New York City real estate values have increased dramatically over the past decades, her surviving husband's estate might be subject to significant estate taxes, which could have been avoided if the estate plan had worked as intended.

The obvious question to be asked of the high-priced attorney handling the matter is why the exact title on the property at issue was never checked by his firm at the time the estate plan was put in place or shortly after the death of his client. It is relatively easy to check the title records related to real estate; the information is even available online these days, so why was that not done?

If it had been discovered shortly after the death of the client that the property was owned as jtwros, it would have been possible for the surviving spouse to sign and file a postmortem disclaimer that could have rectified the problem. Not handling this matter correctly was a big mistake that may ultimately cost my wife and her brother a significant amount of unnecessary estate taxes. But Mr. Big-Shot Attorney would never admit that he had made a mistake in this connection, and my father-in-law was too genteel a person to pursue the matter further. In hindsight, the bigger mistake may be for family members not to use the services of a relative who not only possesses the experience and expertise necessary to render correct legal advice, but also has a financial interest and incentive to minimize estate taxes and estate administration expenses.

Mistake #21: Forgetting That Real Estate Usually Passes Subject to Loans and Mortgages

I t is usually a good thing to be named in a Will as the beneficiary of residential real estate that had been owned by a decedent. But in this current economy, where mortgages sometimes exceed the fair market value of properties, let the beneficiary beware.

Under New York law, and that of most states, when a decedent owned property that has a mortgage or other loan secured by that property at the time of the decedent's death, and devises that property to a particular person under his Will, that real property passes to the beneficiary, subject to the underlying mortgage or loan attached to that property.

The executor of a decedent's estate is not responsible for providing payment for the balance of that loan out of the other property in the decedent's estate. The beneficiary is entitled to have the loan paid from the other assets of the estate *only* if the testator expressly and specifically so states in his Will. A clause or provision in a Will that generally instructs the executor to pay the legal debts of the estate is not sufficient to require that the mortgage or loan on a specifically devised or bequeathed piece of real estate or a cooperative apartment be paid from the other assets of the estate.

Many years ago, my firm represented a client who was the beneficiary of a cash bequest under a Will of a friend. She had been told by the liar, I mean lawyer, for the estate that the amount of her cash legacy was being reduced because of all of the expenses that had to be paid by the executor from the general assets of the estate, which would result in all of the bequests being reduced proportionately. When we examined those expenses in the accounting of the executor, we found that the estate had improperly paid off an outstanding loan on the decedent's cooperative apartment, which had been specifically bequeathed to a person who, it turned out, was the lover of the estate's lover, I mean lawyer. That loan payment was to his lover's benefit, but to the detriment of all of the other beneficiaries of the estate. When we pointed out the mistake to the estate's attorney, and read him the New York law on the subject (and the riot act), he had no choice but to arrange for his lover to reimburse the estate for the full amount of the loan that had been paid off, plus expenses, which had been improperly paid from other estate assets. As a result, our client received the total amount of the bequest provided for her in the Will, with no reduction.

It would have been a mistake for our client not to retain a knowledgeable, experienced and effective attorney to assist her with this matter. And in the case discussed above, it was a mistake for the executor to pay off that loan, and to let the estate's lying, loving lawyer improperly mix business with his pleasure. As a legal lesson, not understanding that inherited real estate often comes with strings, and mortgages, attached is a mistake that can have serious repercussions.

Mistake #22: Not Draining the Water Pipes in a Vacant House in Cold Weather

You've heard the saying, "You might be able to slip something past your mother, but you can't fool Mother Nature." This practical lesson is one that my clients and I learned the hard way. (Note this discussion may apply more to northerners than to southerners because of the differing temperatures during the winter months.)

When a house is occupied, it is being warmed, dishes are being washed and toilets are being flushed. The water in the house is on the move, and the plumber is not required. However, after a person has died, if the house remains vacant, those things do not happen to the same degree, if at all. The heating system may be adjusted downward, or it may fail altogether as the result of an oil or gas burner turning off because of the lack of fuel feeding it. There is no activity in the pipes and the water in the pipes just stays in one place. After a few days of freezing temperatures, the pipes will have no choice but to burst, because ice takes up more space than water does, and even a strong metal pipe can't handle the extra pressure. If you are lucky, only the accessible radiators will burst; if the pipes themselves burst, that could require breaking though floors and walls of the house just to get access to the pipes to replace them. Needless to say, there are no water systems operating while these repairs are going on, and no one wants to buy a house that doesn't have sinks and showers that work. Huge hassle.

The solution appears relatively simple. You can arrange to have all the pipes drained by a plumber before the cold winter months set in, or you can be totally vigilant about monitoring and visiting a house when it is not occupied. But, regardless of how vigilant, the lawyer, executor, or caretaker might be, things do happen.

Mistakes Involving Real Estate

I have had only two estates in more than 25 years of practice where the pipes in the house broke, and it was during the same unusually cold winter. In the first one, the boiler inexplicably stopped working (there was plenty of oil in the tank), and after two or three days of frigid northeastern United States temperatures, the radiators blew. This first story actually had a happy ending, because that estate received an insurance payment, based on our claim filed, that significantly exceeded the actual cost of the repairs. In other words, the estate actually benefited financially and also had an impressive new set of radiators.

In the second instance, freezing pipes enabled an estate I was handling to force the squatting girlfriend of the decedent to vacate the same premises. Years of legal wrangling, and thousands of dollars in legal fees, had not enabled the estate to accomplish what Mother Nature could. Perhaps the squatting girlfriend's money ran out and she just stopped paying to heat that house; Mother Nature took over, and the pipes froze after many cold January nights. That was actually a good result for the estate, which had been trying to work through the legal system to legally evict this squatter for a few years. A few cold days in January helped achieve a result that the court system could not expeditiously resolve, as it is often quite difficult to evict a tenant.

It can be a costly mistake to neglect the water pipes in any vacant properties—residential or commercial. Be sure that the home's water pipes are properly drained before the winter or that there is constant vigilance and monitoring (i.e., washing, flushing, and watering) of the property involved.

Mistake #23: Failing to Maintain Adequate Property and Casualty Insurance on Estate Property—Especially Vacant Real Estate

As the executor or co-administrator of the two estates with the broken pipes, I was lucky under the circumstances. But those were also situations where I made my own luck. What we call *luck* is often the result of doing the right things to set up that good luck. When it comes to handling an estate that owns valuable tangible and real property, bad luck sometimes does happen with the Rembrandt painting or in the cooperative apartment, but that is no excuse for the failure to maintain adequate property and casualty insurance on all estate property that is subject to damage, theft or other casualty loss.

After a person who has left tangible or real property behind dies, someone should contact the decedent's insurance carrier as soon as possible. At that time, this person should advise the carrier of the death of their customer and ensure that insurance coverage continues in full force and without interruption during the administration of the estate.

If the insurance company is not informed of its client's death within a reasonable period, it could deny coverage if a claim is asserted. Usually buried deep in the fine print of every insurance contract are the provisions, which state the duty to advise of an insured's death within a reasonable period of time. What constitutes a "reasonable" period of time may depend on the facts and circumstances of each particular case. Of course, when you report the death of an insured of a life insurance policy, the insurance company may not be as eager to hear from you because that death means that a claim for the payment of life insurance proceeds will be asserted soon.

As mentioned in the story about the broken pipes, the insurance coverage paid to the estate to repair the pipes actually exceeded the final cost of the repairs. As a result, the estate benefitted from that payment. This payment was received because I had advised the insurance agent of the death of his customer shortly after she died. As such, he did what was necessary to allow the executor to step into the high-heeled shoes of the decedent, figuratively but definitely not literally, and receive the insurance proceeds.

The lesson here is that you should be sure to ask your insurance broker for a signed binder or some other proof that the insurance company is on notice of the death of its customer, or you could be setting the executor or administrator up for a big problem and potential liability later.

It is a big mistake not to be sure that an estate continues to maintain, or obtain, sufficient insurance coverage against all the things, natural or unnatural, that can, and often do, go wrong in life (and afterward). If you don't do that, and an estate suffers a loss, the beneficiaries might believe that the executor or administrator should have foreseen that possibility, checked on the insurance, and asked him or her to compensate them from personal funds, and that would be no fun.

Mistake #24: Failing to Provide That Children, or Others, May Continue to Reside in the Family Home with the Executor's or Trustee's Approval

Under ordinary circumstances and planning, an executor or a trustee has a duty to sell non-income-producing assets owned by an estate or a trust. A fiduciary, such as an executor or trustee, is expected to liquidate any and all assets that do not generate revenue for the beneficiaries of the estate. An executor or a trustee can be criticized for failing to do so, and can even meet up with the dreaded Sir Charge, I mean surcharge, imposed on him or her by an angry Surrogate's or Probate Court Judge.

However, suppose that a young mother and father die unexpectedly, leaving their three kids, ages 17, 14, and 9, as their sole surviving beneficiaries. From a psychological standpoint, do you think it is a good idea to remove these three children from their family home right at the moment of their greatest grief? The answer to this question will depend on the particular circumstances of that family and might be different for each child. So, I guess I should leave the answer to the court-appointed guardian ad litem or the child therapist, licensed or otherwise. But, for the sake of learning how to avoid estate planning mistake #24, I am going to shed some light on this situation.

It certainly makes sense to allow the children to stay in their family's home for an extended period of time; however, if their parents' Wills do not expressly allow this, the executors or trustees might believe that they have a duty to sell such non-income producing assets as the home in a relatively short period of time. Indeed, if taxes are due from the estate, he might have to sell that property to raise cash to pay estate taxes and other administration expenses.

It is a mistake not to have a Will or trust that authorizes and empowers the executor or trustee to permit your children to reside in your home or other residential property you may own for whatever period of time that you believe is best. This applies not only to minor children under the age of 18, but also for older children whose share of your estate may be held in trust for them until age 30, 40, or even for their lifetimes. Because the family house might be owned by a trust under the Will, the trustee needs to have clear written "marching" orders in the Will as to the trustee's direction to maintain the family home for the benefit of the children or others, and the clearer that those directions are, the more protected the trustee will be.

The following is some valuable free legal advice, which contains a clause often included in the Wills prepared by my law firm.

> If my wife, OLIVE OIL, shall not survive me, but any child of mine shall survive me, I authorize and empower, but I do not direct, the trustees of the trusts for the benefit of my children created by Article NINTH hereof, in their discretion, to retain any residence or residences (land, houses and other buildings, condominiums, apartments and/or cooperative apartments) and, anything contained in the provisions of Article SECOND hereof to the contrary notwithstanding, any of my tangible personal property located therein or used or of use in connection therewith, as part of the principal of any or all of such trusts and for such period or periods as they deem advisable or proper while such trusts continue, for the benefit of any child of mine, and to:
> 1. Maintain such residence as a home for the benefit of any child or children of mine and the guardians of the person of any minor child or children of mine or any adult designated by such guardians and the family of any such

guardian or adult (hereinafter collectively called "Other Occupants"), and pay such charges for maintenance, taxes, water, assessments, fuel, insurance, repairs (including substantial repairs, alterations and additions), mortgage interest and amortization, and general upkeep, in connection with such residence, from the principal or income of such trusts, as my Trustees, in their discretion, determine;

2. Permit any child or children of mine and such Other. Occupants to occupy such residence and use such tangibles without requiring any of them to pay any rent or other charge for the occupancy or use thereof;

3. Exchange any such residence and/or any of such tangibles for, or sell such residence to any party, including the Trustees hereof, and/or any of such tangibles, and with the proceeds or any part thereof, or with additional funds from the principal of any such trust or trusts, purchase another residence and/or tangibles to be used as or in the home of any such child or children of mine, and permit the occupancy and use thereof as hereinabove provided; and

4. I direct that my Trustees shall be under no liability or obligation for failing to sell or otherwise dispose of such residence and/or such tangibles for the purpose of investing the proceeds of such sale or disposition, or for failure to repair and maintain the same, or for any loss of, damage to or depreciation in value thereof.

In view of the normal obligation of a fiduciary to sell estate assets, it is a mistake not to include a clause in your Will that expressly allows your Executors and/or Trustees to maintain a family home for the benefit of the children or grandchildren and to allow those children to continue to reside in the home rent-free for a specified period of time.

Mistake #25: Failing to Provide That Existing Leases Will Terminate on Reasonable Terms After the Death of the Owner of the Property

I had a 90-year-old client who liked to handle many legal matters herself, even though she was not an attorney. She prepared a lease for a tenant who was to live on the carriage house located on her property. Unfortunately, my client, despite her advanced age, did not include in the terms of the lease agreement executed between herself and her tenant any language concerning what, if any, occupancy rights the tenant might enjoy following her demise.

After my client's very long and full life came to a close, I, as the attorney for her estate and the nominated executor of her Last Will and Testament, was forced to deal with the presence of this tenant and with any consequences that her occupancy might have on my ability to arrange for the property to be sold and the proceeds added to the decedent's distributable estate.

As one might imagine, the presence of a tenant greatly encumbered my ability to sell the property at the highest possible price. The decedent's failure to draft a lease agreement that clearly addressed any rights the aforementioned tenant might have in the event of her death left open the possibility that the tenant might continue to enjoy her occupancy of the rented property for a lengthy period of time.

The presence of the tenant forced me, my firm, and another attorney retained by the estate in connection with the potential sale of the property to devote dozens of hours of our time to resolving an issue that could have been avoided if the decedent had simply added an additional sentence to the "do-it-yourself" lease she had drawn up. As a result of the tenant's continued occupancy, my staff and I were prevented from placing the decedent's townhouse on the market as quickly as we would have liked and lining up potential purchasers. Additionally, we were forced to devote our time to exploring any rights the estate might have, and whether or not the continued occupancy of the pre-existing tenant would force us to pursue those rights through litigation.

I was fortunate to be able to reach an agreement with the tenant and eventually arranged for the decedent's townhouse to be sold for its fair market value. However, this situation should still serve as a warning to individuals, that when entering into lease agreements like the one being discussed here, it is a mistake not to include a provision in any lease that terminates the tenant's right to occupancy at the time of your death, or at some reasonable date thereafter. This is especially important when the leased space is attached to a personal residence, which can usually be counted on to be one of the largest (if not the largest) asset left as part of an estate.

Mistake #26: Owning Land, a House, or an Apartment in a Foreign Country

Unless you are unusually wealthy, it is probably a mistake to own real estate or other residential property in another country, as it may end up causing numerous problems for the executor, administrator, and/or beneficiaries of your estate. That is because every country has its own laws and rules as to what is required for property to pass under a Will, trust, or by intestacy. Whenever you hear about rules and laws, lawyers and judges and courts cannot be far behind. That can lead to trouble with a capital *T*, may be expensive, and can often take a very, very, very long time to resolve.

My law firm recently handled a matter in which a court in Mexico City, Mexico was involved, and I would have felt relieved if it had only been *mañana*. But we had even more problems with an estate that owned a small piece of land in the Bahamas. In that case, it was not better in the Bahamas; due to the expense and complications involved, the estate decided to abandon its claim to that piece of property, which may have been sold three more times by now.

Owning land in another state in the United States can be complicated and require *ancillary probate* in that state, so owning property in another country can be even more complicated. Those complications are even greater after you die and the property is part of your estate. Not only do the requisite taxes and other fees need to continue to be paid, but is it often very difficult to transfer the title of that property into someone else's name. There are a couple of ways to avoid that mess: You may have the property owned in the name of a trust that you have established during your lifetime and that will continue by its own terms after your death, or you may own the property jointly, although that may be more complicated in a foreign jurisdiction than it sounds. The take-away here may be that it is better to rent real property in a foreign country than to own it.

Mistake #27: Assuming That a Co-operative Apartment Building Board Will Always Do What You Would Like

In the great city of New York, many extraordinarily wealthy people live in *co-ops*. That is a shorthand way of stating that the apartment building in which these people live has been organized as a corporation, and each apartment is allocated a proportionate number of shares based on its size and other factors. Because each apartment owner is a shareholder in a corporation, he or she needs to obtain the approval of the Board of Directors of the building, who have been elected by the shareholders, to do almost anything that affects the lives, directly or indirectly, of the other shareholders (owners) in the building.

Every residential real estate broker in New York City will tell you a horror story about a prospective purchaser of an expensive apartment who was "rejected" by the co-op's Board of Directors. Instead of being co-operative, the Boards are often decidedly unco-operative. That failure to co-operate not only costs the broker his anticipated commission on the aborted sale, but also means that the owner/seller of the apartment must start from scratch, relisting the apartment and going through the entire horrible process all over again. It may take months or years to find another purchaser, and the final purchase price might be less than the original price offered.

In the context of an estate, a decedent's co-operative apartment immediately becomes more of a liability than an asset, because it is not being lived in, is not generating income, and has ongoing maintenance and utility expenses that must be paid.

Unless a family member can pass muster with the co-op Board members (whom he or she might have offended as a teenager), the owner of the apartment needs to find a buyer, and quick. The estate taxes, if any, are due nine months from the date of death, and co-op apartments are illiquid assets that often have very significant value for estate tax purposes.

Even if the executor of the Will does everything right, and is able to probate the Will, clear out the apartment, properly distribute all of the decedent's stuff, and find a qualified purchaser within nine months of death, all of those best-laid plans may go astray as a result of a Co-op Board's rejection of the proposed purchaser. Ouch!

It is a naïve mistake to assume that the Board of Directors of a co-operative apartment building will do what you want it to do (and the fancier the building, the riskier that assumption is). Co-op boards are notoriously ready, willing, and able to reject the ready, willing, and able buyer who is prepared to pay a lot of cash for your empty apartment. Furthermore, the Co-op board has the legal right to do whatever it wants, as long as the rejection is not based on impermissible grounds such as race, religion, or nationality, among others.

What is the solution to this problem? It may be to get elected to the Co-op Board yourself, because if you can't beat them (and you are not allowed to beat Co-op board members, no matter how angry they make you), you may just have to join them.

Mistake #28: Placing Real Estate in a Trust Without Checking on the Ramifications of Doing So

There may be good legal and tax reasons to transfer a piece of real estate into an irrevocable or revocable type of trust, but before you do, you need to be sure that you understand all of the ramifications of a lifetime transfer of real estate into a trust of any kind.

Despite the downturn in the real estate market in the first decade of the twenty-first century, the house that you bought in the 1950s for $52,000 may be worth more than two or three million dollars. One of your friends tells you about a special type of trust with a funny name—QPRT—that her lawyer set up for her. She transferred her house into this irrevocable trust and was able to make a gift of the family home to her three children without paying any gift tax. Sounds great, right? Well, maybe it is not so great when it comes to the imposition of capital gains taxes.

It is important to know that when a gift is made, the donee of that gift, including an irrevocable trust that acts as a conduit to the ultimate beneficiaries of the property, takes the gift with the same basis as the donor had in the property. Therefore, when the property is ultimately sold by the beneficiaries, they will have to pay capital gains tax on the difference between the original cost basis (including any capital improvements) and the sale price. Alternatively, if the property had not been transferred during the decedent's lifetime, the decedent's estate would have received a stepped-up basis on the property (i.e., the fair market value of the property as of the date of death), and not the original cost of the property. If the stepped-up basis is utilized, then there will be no capital gains tax payable, because there will be no difference between the sale price and the date of death value—and therefore no capital gain. If the federal exemption for the estate tax continues to be at least $2 million and that house is the only asset in your estate, then you will pay no federal estate tax, and there would be no capital gains tax either. Simply put—if you took your friend's advice, your children or other beneficiaries could end up paying a substantial capital gains tax for no good reason.

If we were to assume a $1.9 million capital gain on the sale, putting that family home into a QPRT or other type of gifting could be a $285,000 mistake. Be sure that you understand, and that your lawyer understands and explains, all of the implications, tax and otherwise, when you are transferring the title of real estate into a trust, even if you are doing it with the best of intentions.

Mistakes Involving Executors and/or Trustees

Perhaps the single most important decision you can make when it comes to estate planning is your choice as to who will handle things after you are gone. The person who will execute the terms of the Will is called an *executor* in most states and a *personal representative* in some others. His or her role is to collect the decedent's assets, pay the decedent's bills and taxes, if any, and then to fulfill the terms of the Will. It is often a very big and thankless job, and the many celebrities whose stories are told in the following chapter did not always make the best decisions when it came to their choice of executors and trustees.

Whether it is too many or too few executors and/or trustees, the wrong choices can lead to disaster, as illustrated by the estate planning mistakes and stories involving some of the rich and famous that are discussed in this chapter.

Mistake #29: Selecting Only One Executor in a Complicated Estate

Certain estates do require and would benefit from the services of multiple executors. For example, if the estate has substantial, diverse, and complicated assets, it may be beneficial to have more than one executor making the numerous decisions. That advice was not followed in the estate of the great 20th-century artist Andy Warhol, who died with a multifaceted estate valued at Warhol's death in 1987 at more than $500 million.[1]

Andy Warhol's vast estate included real estate and homes in various places, including New York City, Montauk, and Colorado. He also owned *Interview* magazine, jewelry, watches, cigar-store Indians, lots and lots of art made by him and his many artist friends, and a very large collection of cookie jars. There was a lot of stuff to worry about, and it was probably too much for one man, even if that one man was Frederick Hughes, Warhol's long time business manager and the person who gave Andy mouth-to-mouth resuscitation when Warhol was shot by a deranged former Factory worker in 1968. Warhol obviously trusted Hughes, but may not have taken into account that Fred Hughes was afflicted with multiple sclerosis, which may have made it physically difficult for him to fulfill his fiduciary obligations. The Warhol estate was embroiled in all kinds of litigation as a result of decisions made by the sole executor.

In 2001, Fred Hughes died at the young age of 57, 14 years after Warhol. As the sole executor of Warhol's estate, Frederick Hughes was paid a substantial executor's commission that, in accordance with New York law and the size of the Warhol estate, may have exceeded $10 million. Good work, if you can get it.

But there is a very important reason to have more than one executor when an estate is large and has numerous valuable assets:

checks and balances. It is often beneficial to have at least two executors, and preferably an odd number (see Mistake #31), so that they can keep an eye on one another. It may be easier for one person to embezzle than two. If two or more executors participate in something improper or criminal, then there is a conspiracy; that may be less likely to occur than a single executor with his or her hand in the proverbial "cookie jar," even if the estate, like Andy Warhol's, had hundreds of them.

Mistake #30: Selecting Too Many Executors

Although it is beneficial to have more than one executor to handle a complicated or potentially problematic estate, sometimes the desire to have more than one executor can be taken too far to the other extreme.

William Paley, who died at the age of 89 in 1990, was called in his *New York Times* obituary a "20th-century visionary with the ambitions of a 19th-century robber baron."[2] He died with a vast estate that was valued at around $500 million and included a large block of stock in the communications empire that he built, CBS, as well as a large collection of 19th- and 20th-century art, which he bequeathed to New York's Museum of Modern Art.

William S. Paley had a 75-page Will that he signed in 1985, and 16 subsequent codicils, or amendments, to that Will, with the last codicil being signed on July 30, 1990, shortly before he died in October. It is not simple to parse through the Will and codicils to determine the final terms of Paley's Last Will and Testament, but Paley's estate's law firm, Cravath, Swaine & Moore, assembled a consolidated Last Will and Testament (see Exhibit 4.1), which was filed with the Surrogate's Court to help the probate department clerks (and public record seekers like me).

Paley felt the need to name six individuals to handle his estate. These trusted executors included former Secretary of State Henry Kissinger; famed Paul, Weiss, Rifkind, Wharton & Garrison; attorney Arthur L. Liman; business executives; and one big bank, Morgan Guaranty Trust Company of New York. In view of the importance of the executors, it is clear that Bill Paley didn't fall prey to Mistake #29, but with a high-powered group of seven executors, it must not have been too easy to schedule meetings or reach a consensus. A situation

CONSOLIDATED LAST WILL AND TESTAMENT
OF WILLIAM S. PALEY

I, WILLIAM S. PALEY, of New York, New York,
declare this to be my last will and testament.

FIRST: I revoke all wills and codicils which I
have heretofore made.

SECOND: 1/ (A) (1) I appoint JOHN S. MINARY,
SIDNEY W. HARL, FRANK STANTON, ARTHUR L. LIMAN, HENRY A.
KISSINGER, PATRICK S. GALLAGHER and, subject to the provi-
sions of Article EIGHTEENTH hereof, MORGAN GUARANTY TRUST
COMPANY OF NEW YORK as executors of this will.

(2) Upon the first of John S. Minary, Sidney W.
Harl, Frank Stanton, Arthur L. Liman, Henry A. Kissinger and
Patrick S. Gallagher to fail to take office or cease to
serve as an executor of this will, I appoint DANIEL L.
MOSLEY as an executor of this will.

(B) (1) I appoint SIDNEY W. HARL, JOHN S.
MINARY, ARTHUR L. LIMAN, HENRY A. KISSINGER, PATRICK S.
GALLAGHER and, subject to the provisions of Article EIGHT-
EENTH hereof, MORGAN GUARANTY TRUST COMPANY OF NEW YORK as
trustees of each trust created hereunder other than the
trust created under Article EIGHTH hereof.

(2) Upon the first of Sidney W. Harl, John S.
Minary, Arthur L. Liman, Henry A. Kissinger and Patrick S.
Gallagher to fail to take office or cease to serve as a

1/Subdivision (A), (B) and (C) of Article SECOND were
amended by the fourth, fifth, sixth, seventh, eleventh,
twelfth and fifteenth codicils to Mr. Paley's will dated
September 23, 1987, February 25, 1988, June 23, 1988,
October 28, 1988, June 20, 1989, August 3, 1989, and
June 19, 1990, respectively.

Exhibit 4.1 Excerpt from the Consolidated Last Will and Testament of William S. Paley

Source: William S. Paley, Will dated July 31, 1985, Surrogate's Court County of New York, New York, NY.

trustee of any trust created hereunder (other than the trust created under Article EIGHTH hereof), I appoint DANIEL L. MOSLEY as a trustee of such trust.

(3) In making the provisions specified in this Subdivision, it is my wish (but not my direction) that there be at all times at least two individuals serving as trustees of each trust created hereunder other than the trust created under Article EIGHTH hereof.

(4) If at any time there shall be fewer than two individual trustees of any trust other than the trust created under Article EIGHTH hereof then in office, I appoint as a trustee of such trust such individual as shall be designated by the then presiding partner of Cravath, Swaine & Moore (or its successor), with the prior written consent to such designation of a majority of my adult descendents who shall then be living and able to act. Upon qualifying as provided by law, the individual so designated shall become a trustee hereunder as though originally named herein.

(C) (1) I appoint JOHN S. MINARY, SIDNEY W. HARL and PATRICK S. GALLAGHER as trustees of the trust created under Article EIGHTH hereof. If at any time there shall be no person serving as a trustee of such trust, I appoint MORGAN GUARANTY TRUST COMPANY OF NEW YORK as trustee of such trust.

(2) Morgan Guaranty Trust Company of New York or any other bank or trust company serving hereunder at any time as coexecutor or cotrustee is hereinafter sometimes referred to as the "Corporate Fiduciary".

(D) Notwithstanding the foregoing provisions of this Article, no individual appointed as an executor hereof

Exhibit 4.1 (*Continued*)

100

like this can prove problematic, as estate administration decisions sometimes have to be made very quickly without the opportunity to consult and deliberate.

Tough businessman that he was, Paley also provided that the seven executors should all share one-fourth of a single executor's commission. Based on applicable New York law, and assuming a $500 million estate, each executor would have been entitled to a reduced executor's fee of approximately $350,000. Paley must have believed that the honor of acting as one of his executors should have been worth something. And none of the seven named chose to renounce his appointment, so Bill Paley obviously knew what he was doing.

For a complicated estate with substantial assets, it is sensible to name multiple executors, but Bill Paley's appointment of seven may have gone a little too far. Perhaps three and five were just channels that Bill Paley chose not to watch. From a practical point of view, it may be a mistake to name so many executors that it is difficult to schedule meetings or have documents signed by all of the required executors.

Mistake #31: Selecting an Even Number of Executors

Suppose the executors of your Will disagree on some aspect of the administration of your estate or the execution of your Will. Since each executor normally has one vote, you may have an intractable problem if you have an even number of executors. As many states provide that the majority rules when it comes to fiduciaries (i.e., executors or trustees), it may be advisable to have an odd number of executors. Having an odd number can potentially avoid a stalemate, deadlock, or logjam that could result in the disputing executors going to court to resolve their differences. Going to court can be time consuming and expensive.

As mentioned throughout this book, the choice of the executor or executors of your Will is a critical one. Care should be taken to be sure that two, four, six, or eight Executors don't run into an administrative nightmare. This potential problem can easily be avoided by remembering the benefit of a tie breaking voter—an odd number.

Mistake #32: Selecting Executors with a Conflict of Interest

Besides being one of the greatest painters of the 20th century, the abstract expressionist artist Mark Rothko also left an estate that became synonymous with the term "conflict of interest." Although he avoided Mistake #31 by appointing three executors of his Will—Bernard J. Reis, the accountant for Rothko's art dealer, Marlborough Gallery; Theodoros Stamos, an artist who showed at the Marlborough Gallery; and Morton Levine, an anthropology professor who had little to do with Rothko's art world—he failed to consider their inherent conflict of interests. Unfortunately for Professor Levine, the two executors with connections in the art world constituted a majority of the named executors and consequently called the shots. Their decision to sell Rothko's paintings at a deeply discounted price to the Marlborough Gallery was highly criticized; and as a result, all three executors were subsequently removed and surcharged by the New York County Surrogate's Court.[3]

Mark Rothko signed his simple two-page Will in September 1968, less than two years before his death by suicide in February 1970 (see Exhibit 4.2).

The New York County Surrogate's court proceedings, known as "Matter of Rothko," were concluded seven years later, when Surrogate Millard Midonick voided all of the estate's contracts with the Marlborough Gallery, ordered that many valuable paintings be returned to the estate, and ordered that the three conflicted and self-dealing executors be removed and surcharged nine million dollars. Rothko's daughter, Kate, was named as the sole administrator of his estate. She and her younger brother Christopher received about one-half of the estate's holdings, and the other half was distributed to museums around the world by the Mark Rothko Foundation.

LAST WILL AND TESTAMENT
of
MARK ROTHKO

I, MARK ROTHKO, of New York, N. Y. being of sound mind and memory, hereby make, publish and declare this to be my Last Will and Testament, hereby revoking all wills and other testamentary dispositions by me at any time heretofore made.

FIRST: I direct my Executors to pay all my just debts, funeral and administration expenses as soon after my decease as is convenient.

SECOND: I give and bequeath to the TATE GALLERY, London, England, five (5) paintings of their choice of those paintings which were created by me for the Seagram Building, New York in 1959.

THIRD: I give, devise and bequeath to my wife, MARY ALICE, the real estate owned by me at 118 East 95th Street, New York, together with all of the contents thereof.

FOURTH: I hereby bequeath to my wife, MARY ALICE, the sum of Two Hundred Fifty Thousand ($250,000) Dollars.

FIFTH: In the event of the death of my wife or the simultaneous death of myself and my wife, I give, devise and bequeath the sum of Two Hundred Fifty Thousand ($250,000) Dollars, together with the real property at 118 East 95th Street, New York, and all the contents thereof, in equal shares to my children, KATE and CHRISTOPHER.

1.

Exhibit 4.2 The complete Last Will and Testament of Mark Rothko
Source: Mark Rothko, Will dated September 13, 1968, proved April 27, 1970, File Number 1970-1368, Surrogate's Court, New York County, New York, NY.

SIXTH: All the rest, residue and remainder of my property, I give and bequeath to the MARK ROTHKO FOUNDATION, a non-profit organization, incorporated under the laws of the State of New York. The Directors of the Foundation are to be: William Rubin, ROBERT GOLDWATER, BERNARD J. REIS, THEODOROS STAMOS and MORTON LEVINE.

SEVENTH: In the event of the death of my wife or the simultaneous death of my wife and myself, I appoint as Guardians of my children, MR. and MRS. MORTON LEVINE, of New York.

EIGHTH: I hereby nominate, constitute and appoint MORTON LEVINE, BERNARD J. REIS and THEODOROS STAMOS as Executors of this will. I direct that my Executors shall not be required to furnish any bond, undertaking or security for the faithful performance of their duties. In the event of the death of either one or two of them, the remaining person or persons shall serve as Executor.

IN WITNESS WHEREOF, I have hereunto set my hand and seal this 13th day of September, 1968. _Mark Rothko_ (L.S.)

On the 13th day of September, 1968, the above-named Testator, MARK ROTHKO, in our presence, subscribed and sealed the foregoing instrument, and at the time of such subscription, published and declared the same to be his Last Will and Testament, and thereupon we at such time, at the request of the above-named Testator, in his presence, and in the presence of each other, signed our names thereto as subscribing witnesses.

Louis Meyer residing at 64-50 Utopia Parkway, Flushy, NYC 1365

Mary Ann Harte residing at 2441 Webb Ave. Bronx, New York

Ruth B. Miller residing at 222 West 83rd St. NY NY 10024

2.

Surrogate's Court, County of New York

Be it remembered, that in pursuance of Section 1422 of the Surrogate's Court Procedure Act, I hereby certify that on the _27_ day of _April_, 19_70_ the last will and testament of _Mark Rothko_, deceased, being the foregoing written instrument, was upon due proof duly admitted to probate by the Surrogate's Court of the County of New York, and by the Surrogate of said county, as and for the last will and testament_____ of said deceased, and as a will valid to pass _real and personal_ property. Said last will and testament _____recorded in the office of said Surrogate in liber _2758_ of wills, page _485_

In testimony whereof, I have subscribed my name and affixed the seal of office of the Surrogate of said county, this _9_ day of _June_ one thousand nine hundred and _seventy_

William S. Mullen

Clerk of the Surrogate's Court

Exhibit 4.2 (*Continued*)

Remember, it is a big mistake to select executors who may have a conflict of interest with your last wishes or with their co-executors. Therefore, please take this advice into account when selecting your executor or executors.

Mistake # 33: Not Compensating (or Under-Compensating) Your Executors

Although she established a $12-million trust fund for her pet dog Trouble, Leona Helmsley expressly stated in her Will that the five named executors—her brother Alvin Rosethal, her grandsons David Panzirer and Walter Panzirer, her lawyer Sandor Frankel, and her friend John Codey—were not entitled "to statutory commissions" for serving as an executor of, or trustee under, Leona's Will. It is noteworthy and perhaps revealing that Leona refers to only one of the five named executors as her "friend." However, with friends who do not compensate friends for doing a big job, who needs enemies?

Being an executor of a Will entails a large amount of work. Being an executor of Leona Helmsley's Will, and administering her humongous estate, entails a humongous amount of work and a great amount of "exposure" as well. What do I mean by "exposure?" Whenever a person has a fiduciary duty in connection with a trust or any estate, that person is legally responsible for the preservation, and growth, of the assets under his or her control. If the value of the assets decreases or even stays flat, the beneficiaries of an estate will often complain that the executor or trustee was not minding the store properly. When you have billions of dollars of assets—including real estate, operating businesses, art, furniture, jewelry, and dog toys—the potential problems for an executor or a trustee are magnified a billion times. Who needs the aggravation, especially if you are not being paid for it?

Leona's Will was prepared by a lawyer who was apparently in Leona's favor on the day, hour, and minute that she signed her Last

Will and Testament, and he does not leave himself totally out in the cold, as the Will provides:

> Any one or more executors or trustees may render services to the Estate or any Trust hereunder as an officer, manager, or employee of the Estate or any Trust hereunder, or in any other capacity, notwithstanding the fact that they may appoint themselves to serve in such capacities, and they shall be entitled to receive reasonable compensation for such services . . . [4]

As evidenced by the clause above, Leona's lawyer is covered for his services to be rendered, but what about Leona's one named "friend" and her two grandsons? What type of services would they render to the estate that was separate and apart from their fiduciary duties as the executors? (It is noteworthy that Leona's Will initially capitalizes the words "Estate" and "Trusts," but keeps the titles of executor and trustee in the lower case, with the other "little people" to whom Leona had so infamously once referred in connection with her tax evasion conviction.)

So if a person is not being paid for all of the aggravation related to the administration of an estate, what is the incentive for spending much of his or her time working on it? Leona made a mistake by not compensating her executors in accordance with the New York statute, which establishes a formula for determining the executors' commissions. This statute states that two full commissions are to be divided among two or more executors. Even if Leona could not stomach the statutory commission amount, which on a large estate is a very significant amount of compensation, New York would have allowed her to provide some lesser formula or fixed amount.

The five named executors all undoubtedly had better, more lucrative things to do than working for free for the late Leona. It could be expected that the administration of her estate would be delayed and suffer as a result. Alternatively, executors who know that they will be remunerated at the conclusion of the estate administration have a strong incentive to handle the estate administration as expeditiously as possible.

As a consequence of her tightfisted approach to things, Leona may have shot herself in the foot by believing that her grandsons, friend, and lawyer would move as quickly as they did when she was still around cracking her whip. It is often true that you get what you pay for, so it is a mistake not to pay for the services of the executors of your Will. Perhaps Leona believed that paying executors' commissions was only for the "little people."

Mistake #34: **Not Selecting Your Spouse as an Executor**

Although there is no legal requirement that you name your spouse as an executor of your Will, it is increasingly common for spouses to name each other as the sole or one of multiple executors of their respective Wills. In fact, it is more the exception than the rule not to name your wife or husband as your executor. Not surprisingly, many states give the surviving spouse the priority of being appointed as the administrator of the other's estate if there is no Will. Of course, it is also possible for a husband and wife to have waived his or her right to be named as the administrator or executor of the Will of the other in a prenuptial or postnuptial agreement.

It can be perceived as a "slap in the face" to exclude your spouse from making the decisions about issues that will directly affect him or her after your demise. In a time of grief, it may be very difficult for a spouse to feel comfortable discussing highly personal matters with a person named as the executor of your Will, if that person is not related to you. Perhaps it might be even more uncomfortable if that person is related to you, but you do not want him or her to know about your personal financial situation and affairs.

As the rights of, and respect for, women gradually increased over the course of the twentieth century, it was increasingly common for men to name their wives as an executor of their Wills or as a trustee of their trusts. The fact is that in the late twentieth century, and in many societies around the world, women often rule. Ask Margaret Thatcher, Golda Meir, and Indira Gandhi. Closer to home, how about the power of Secretary of State Hillary Clinton from New York and Senator Diane Feinstein of California, Speaker of the House Nancy Pelosi, Congresswomen Nita Lowey and Jane

Harmon, and let's not forget Connecticut's Governor Jodi Rell. With women having firmly established their equality with men on every level, there is no reason to believe that women would not handle the responsibilities of being an executor or trustee as well as, if not better than, their male counterparts.

For a variety of reasons, it may be a mistake not to name your spouse as the executor of your Will—and, of course, also naming a successor executor to your spouse in case he or she is not able to complete the task.

Mistake #35: Surprising Your Spouse with the Terms of Your Will

Having read the last few pages of this chapter, you may now agree that it is a good idea to name your spouse as the sole executor, or one of the group of executors, of your Will. Don't you think that it would also be a good idea for her to know and agree with the terms of the Will that she is being asked to execute and enforce? Suppose the Will provides that all of your assets are to be placed in a lifetime trust for your spouse. She may not like that, and may have every reason and the ability to delay or ignore the terms of your Will because she, right or wrong, believes that the provisions of your Will are not in her best interests. You should be sure that the executor or executors will enforce the terms of your Will, and it may be a good idea to discuss your intentions with your executors before you are no longer around to answer their questions or assuage their concerns.

There may be a variety of things that your executor does not want to do despite the fact that it is specified in your Will. She may not want to pay the bequest or fund the trust specified for your child from a prior marriage. She may not even want to fund the credit shelter trust that was established in your Will for good and sound estate tax reasons, because she does not like the notion of having any of her funds locked up in trust or having to ask the permission of an "independent" trustee to invade principal. An executor can delay the administration of an estate or the funding of the trusts under a Will for months or even years. It is important to consider whether there is a rational, or irrational, reason that your designated executor may not want to do something that your Will directs that he or she must do.

It may be a mistake not to discuss the terms of your Will in advance with your designated executor or executors. Have the discussion now to avoid any unhappy surprises when the terms of your Last Will and Testament are revealed, and you are no longer around to provide commentary and direct traffic.

Mistake #36: Not Naming Your Children as Executors

When there is no surviving spouse available to name as an executor of your Will, you may have no choice but to put your children in charge of your affairs after you are gone. That may be anathema to many to who feel that their children are not the appropriate people to step into their shoes after their deaths; however, as your offspring, your children are apt to know how to handle your financial affairs. After all, you probably raised them with the same values to which you ascribed during your life. Therefore, I urge you not to fall victim to Mistake #36. Name your children as executors of your Will.

For example, despite the fact that she was a widow and had two children who were both attorneys admitted to practice in the state of her domicile, Jackie Kennedy Onassis chose not to name Caroline or John as her executors, but instead appointed an attorney named Forger and a boyfriend named Templesman. Perhaps Jackie felt that her children would have been too grief-stricken to properly fulfill the numerous obligations of an executor of a Will. It has been reported that Caroline and John were not happy that their mother did not name them as executors of her Will, especially in view of the fact that the executors' commissions on an estate the size of Jackie's would have been quite substantial.

Regardless of whether this report is true or not, not naming your children as executors of your Will can lead to ill will (pardon the pun) or feelings of resentment after your death. Therefore, I urge you to heed my advice and name your children to this position.

Mistake #37: Naming Your Children as Executors

On the other hand, sometimes it is a mistake to name your children as the executors of your Will. The reality is that parents and their children do not always get along too well. Very often, parents may, overtly or covertly, disapprove of a lifestyle choice that their child has made that is different from their own.

Take for example, billionaire heiress Doris Duke. Late in her life, at age 75, Duke adopted a 35-year-old woman named Charlene ("Chandi") Gail Heffner, who was reportedly a former devotee of the Hare Krishna religious sect. Within a few years, the adoption went sour and Duke distanced herself from Heffner and expressly disinherited her in her Will as follows:

> TWENTY-ONE: As indicated in Article SEVEN, it is my intention that Chandi Heffner not be deemed to be my child for purposes of disposing of property under this my Will (or any Codicil thereto). Furthermore, it is not my intention, nor do I believe that it was ever my father's intention, that Chandi Heffner be deemed to be a child or lineal descendant of mine for purposes of disposing of the trust estate of the May 2, 1917 trust which my father established for my benefit or the Doris Duke Trust, dated December 11, 1924, which my father established for the benefit of me, certain other members of the Duke family and ultimately for charity.
>
> I am extremely troubled by the realization that Chandi Heffner may use my 1988 adoption of her (when she was 35 years old) to attempt to benefit financially under the terms of either of the trusts created by my father. After giving the matter prolonged and serious consideration, I am convinced that

I should not have adopted Chandi Heffner. I have come to the realization that her primary motive was financial gain. I firmly believe that, like me, my father would not have wanted her to have benefited [sic] under the trusts which he created, and similarly, I do not wish her to benefit from my estate. Accordingly, I specifically authorize and direct my Executors to steadfastly take any and all actions and to expend such funds as my Executors in their sole discretions deem appropriate in order to prove the validity of this my will for the purpose of having it admitted to probate. I also specifically authorize and direct my Executors to steadfastly take any and all action and to expend such funds as my Executors in their sole discretions shall deem advisable in order to prove the effective exercise of the power of appointment described in Article SEVEN of this my will over the principal and income of the trust created by my father, J.B. Duke, as Grantor and Trustee, dated May 2, 1917.[5]

Doris Duke had also made the mistake of naming her butler to be an executor of her Will. Despite the emphatic and express language disinheriting Chandi Heffner, Chandi's attorneys commenced twentieth-century warfare, known as litigation, and were able to extract a settlement from the Duke estate of more than $65 million.

For a variety of reasons, including immaturity, substance or alcohol abuse, Hara Krishna cult influence, or merely being financially unsophisticated or uninterested, there may be many good reasons not to name your child as the sole or even one of the executors of your Will, and it would be a mistake to do so.

Mistake #38: Naming a Literary Executor in Your Will

Although writers do not often write the most interesting Wills for themselves, many of them are concerned about their literary legacy, and name a *literary executor* to deal with and handle the literary property that is part of their estate. There is no specific statutory authority in most states for a literary executor, but a testator can direct that a particular individual (in the capacity of executor) make the final decisions relating to all matters involving the literary property in an estate. This approach is an effective means to centralize and unify the management of literary assets, especially when there are multiple beneficiaries.

Susan Sontag—social commentator, critic, activist and acclaimed writer—executed her Last Will and Testament six months before she died on December 28, 2004 at age 71. She appointed her only son David as the sole executor of her Will, but also expressly appointed her son David and her literary agent, Andrew Wylie, as literary executors. The exact language used in Sontag's 2004 Last Will and Testament appointing her executor and literary executors is reproduced in Exhibit 4.3.

Unfortunately, because the term "literary executor" is not found or defined in the applicable New York statute, letters testamentary were not issued to Mr. Wylie by the Surrogate's Court, and his appointment was a matter of "form over substance," according to the attorney at the fancy law firm that prepared Sontag's Will.

Sontag's Will states that both David and her literary agent, Andrew Wylie, shall serve as her literary executors, without compensation, but with broad "rights, powers, authorities, and privileges with respect to 'my literary property.'" However, the decree granting probate of the Sontag Will makes no mention of any literary executor, and names Sontag's son as the sole executor of her Will.

Mistakes Involving Executors and/or Trustees

SIXTH:

A. I appoint my son, DAVID SONTAG RIEFF, as Executor of my Will. If my said son or any substitute or successor to him shall fail to qualify or cease to act, I appoint as Executor such individual as the last Executor to act shall designate.

B. I appoint my son, DAVID SONTAG RIEFF, and ANDREW WYLIE as Literary Executors with respect to my literary property, including my copyrights, royalty agreements, manuscripts, notes, papers and other writings of which I am the author. I confer upon my Literary Executors the powers enumerated in Article Eighth hereof to make proper arrangement for the publication of my literary property and to take such other actions as may be proper and necessary for the promotion of such literary property. Upon the death of either of my said son or said Andrew Wylie, or in the event that either should resign or be unable to act as such Literary Executor, the other shall act alone. I direct that my Literary Executors shall serve without compensation.

Exhibit 4.3 Excerpt from the Will of Susan Sontag

Source: Susan Sontag, Will dated June 9, 2004, proved January 18, 2005, File Number 2005-0129, Surrogate's Court, County of New York, New York, NY.

The concept of a literary executor is not a new one, and in 1950 a New York court ruled that "while there is no such thing as 'literary executor' under New York law, a person may be designated executor solely for the purpose of administering literary property." Thus, the preferred way to appoint a literary executor may be to petition for letters testamentary to be issued to all nominated executors, but limiting the so-called literary executor's authority to act on matters involving the decedent's literary property only. The decree granting probate of Sontag's will, however, makes no mention of limited letters testamentary or limited letters of trusteeship being issued to her literary executors, because her entire estate was left outright to her son.

Another way to handle the desire to involve a literary fiduciary would be for a Will to explicitly place all literary property into a separate class or trust to be administered by a special literary executor or trustee. Yet Sontag's Will does not do this. Instead, her Will directs that after her tangible personal property is disposed of, her remaining property is to be bequeathed as part of her residuary estate.

The estate of writer Lillian Hellman, who died in 1984, is another example of a Will that did not properly address the role of a literary property executor. The central issue was "whether the testatrix bequeathed right, title and interest to her literary works to the literary property fiduciaries . . . or whether her literary property rights fall into her residuary estate." While Lillian Hellman's Will spelled out the duties, compensation, and specific powers of the literary property fiduciaries, these fiduciaries were not explicitly given a trust to administer (although there were other testamentary trusts created by her will).

In construing the Hellman Will, the New York County Surrogate's Court stated that an implied trust could be considered, but that "bestowing the mantle of traditional trustee upon the literary property fiduciaries does not adequately reflect the special burdens imposed by a literary property res." Accordingly, the court ordered the issuance of limited letters of trusteeship under SCPA section 702(8), and held the literary property fiduciaries to be trustees for the limited purpose of taking title to the literary property and managing it in accordance with one of the testamentary trusts under the testatrix's Will.

If the literary property is placed in trust, the trustee would be the obvious choice to be the fiduciary responsible for the literary property. If the property is held by the estate, then during the period of administration, one or more of the executors should be specifically empowered. The executors also might consider keeping one of themselves in power after the basic estate administration has been completed to renew copyrights in the ensuing years and handle any future claims or offers.

When it comes to literary property in an estate, it is a mistake not to consult with experienced and expert trusts and estates counsel to deal with the complicated issues that arise related to that special form of property.

Mistake #39: Naming a Corporate Fiduciary That Can Be Removed by an Individual Fiduciary

The estate planning of the poor little rich girl, Doris Duke, is a textbook example of Mistake #39—why you should not name a corporate executor that can be removed at the sole discretion of the individual executor of your Will.

When Doris Duke was 12 years old, her father died, and she inherited approximately $50 million in the middle of the Roaring Twenties. Doris Duke continued to roar until her death at age 80. At the time of Doris Duke's death in 1993, her estate was worth approximately $1.2 billion. Duke's substantial assets included large homes like "Shangri La" in Kaalawai, Hawaii; "Falcon's Lair" in Beverly Hills, California; a penthouse on Park Avenue in New York City; and "Rough Point" in Newport, Rhode Island. Despite those exotic options, Duke's legal domicile (i.e., single primary legal residence) at the time of her death was her 2,700-acre estate in the great state of New Jersey. In view of the protracted and expensive legal machinations in the New York County Surrogate's Court, Duke's original estate attorneys might have been well-advised to probate Duke's Will in her local New Jersey court, rather than crossing the Hudson River to the Big Apple.

Most of her vast estate was given to a variety of charities and private foundations of Duke's own creation, including the Doris Duke Foundation for the Preservation of New Jersey Farmland and Farm Animals; the Doris Duke Foundation for the Preservation of Endangered Wildlife; the Doris Duke Foundation for Southeast Asian Art and Culture; and, last but not least, the Doris Duke Foundation for Islamic Art. In the case of the Foundation for the Preservation of Endangered Wildlife, Duke directed that it use its resources to provide an enclosure "to protect endangered species of all kinds, both flora and fauna, from becoming extinct."

However, Doris Duke made the mistake of naming her butler to be the executor of her Will. If ever there were a case where the butler may indeed have "done it," this may be the one. Bernard Lafferty began as Duke's butler and became her closest confidante in the final years of her life. The semiliterate, profligate, imprudent Lafferty was named as the sole individual executor, and he also was given the authority to select a corporate co-trustee to act with him. That broad discretion may have lead to the serious legal problems that plagued the Duke estate from the "get-go."

During the course of his supposed "stewardship" of the Duke estate, Mr. Lafferty did things such as have the estate buy a brand new Cadillac to replace the one that he himself had "totaled." He charged his personal credit card bills with ZIP code–like monthly amounts to the estate, and he spared little expense. He renovated Doris Duke's bedroom into his own. The Surrogate's Court decisions involving him read almost like a criminal indictment, with allegations including: "Commingling of Estate and Personal Assets," "Self-Dealing," "Waste of Estate Assets," "Improvidence and Want of Understanding," and "Substance Abuse."[6] Ultimately, the legal and capitalist system worked. After protracted and expensive legal wrangling, Mr. Lafferty was removed as co-executor, and surrendered his seat on the Duke Foundation Boards. Yet he was awarded a substantial severance package in excess of $5 million. Unfortunately, things did not get better for Mr. Lafferty. Life in the fast lane caught up with him, and he himself died on November 4, 1996 at the young age of 51.[7] We don't know whether former butler Lafferty had a chance to spend all of the Duke dough in the six months between the settlement and his death, but he certainly was a man who knew how to enjoy many of the finer things in life, and he may have died trying.

Duke made a big mistake by selecting an executor who did not have the requisite skills, experience, or temperament to handle the administration of her complicated estate. Duke compounded that mistake by allowing that individual executor to have the right to discharge and change the corporate executor of her Will.

If you want the stability and continuity that a corporate fiduciary would provide, then it is not sensible for the individual fiduciary to have the right and discretion to discharge and change that corporate fiduciary, and Doris Duke's fancy attorneys should have advised their enormously wealthy client not to allow that in her problematic Last Will and Testament.

Notes

1. Andy Warhol, Will dated March 11, 1982, File Number 1987-0824, Surrogate's Court, County of New York, New York, NY.
2. "William S. Paley, Builder of CBS, Dies at 89," *New York Times*, October 27, 1990.
3. Mark Rothko, Will dated September 13, 1968, proved April 27, 1970, File Number 1970-1368, Surrogate's Court, New York County, New York, NY.
4. Leona Helmsley, Will dated July 15, 2005, proved March 21, 2008, File Number 2968-2007, Surrogate's Court, County of New York, New York, NY.
5. Doris Duke, Will dated April 5, 1993, proved May 15, 1996, File Number 4440-1993, Surrogate's Court, County of New York, New York, NY.
6. Doris Duke, Order dated May 22, 1995, File Number 4440-1993, Surrogate's Court, County of New York, New York, NY.
7. "Bernard Lafferty, the Butler For Doris Duke, Dies at 51," *New York Times*, November 5, 1996, pp. B8.

CHAPTER 5

Mistakes Involving Guardians, Minors, or Step-Children

As important as the choice of executors and trustees may be, for a parent there is usually no bigger and more difficult decision than who to select as the guardian of your minor child if both you and the child's other parent die before the child reaches the age of majority. In this chapter, I will discuss the estate planning mistakes that pertain to naming guardians in your Will. In doing so, I will discuss examples of mistakes that Anna Nicole Smith and John Lennon made in their estate planning documents, and also showing Natalie Wood's thoughtfulness and concern for her children.

Mistake #40: Not Naming the Biological Parent as the Guardian of Your Minor Children

It may seem obvious that a child's biological father or mother has the first priority to be the legal guardian of his or her minor children, but sometimes people try to skirt or circumvent the legal reality. It is a mistake not to accept the reality of the parentage of your child and try to overcome that with an ineffective statement in your ineffective Will.

The 2001 Will of former Playboy Playmate of the Year and professional stripper Anna Nicole Smith (whose legal name was Vickie Lynn Marshall, but who was also known as Vickie Lynn Smith and Vickie Lynn Hogan) states the following in connection with the "Office of Guardian" at the bottom of page 13 of her Will in Exhibit 5.1.

Not only was Smith's personal attorney and boyfriend Howard Stern named as the guardian of "the person of my minor child DANIEL WAYNE SMITH," but Stern was also named as the "successor guardian." Why would a person be appointed both guardian and successor guardian? Does that mean that if Howard had died and been reincarnated, he could then act as the successor to himself? What were Anna Nicole and her attorneys thinking when they drafted that bizarre clause?

As things ultimately worked out, or in, as it were, the guardian of Anna Nicole's surviving six-month-old daughter was eventually that daughter's father, Larry Birkhead. Mr. Birkhead was a photographer who obviously got some up-close and personal shots with Anna Nicole, as the DNA and paternity tests conducted after Ms. Smith died conclusively proved. Mr. Birkhead was adjudicated to be the baby girl's father, and not the Stern man who had been trying to raise the baby as his own and had been named the guardian

indirectly, contests or attacks this Will or the Trust or any of the provisions of said instruments, or conspires with or assists anyone in any such contest, or pursues any creditor's claim that my Executor reasonably deems to constitute a contest, any share or interest in my estate or the Trust given to that contesting beneficiary under this Will or the Trust is revoked and shall be disposed of as if the contesting beneficiary had predeceased me without descendants, and shall augment proportionately the shares of my estate passing to or in trust for my beneficiaries who have not participated in such acts. This Article shall not apply to a disclaimer. Expenses to resist a contest or other attack of any nature shall be paid from my estate as expenses of administration.

6.2. General Disinheritance.

Except as otherwise provided herein and in the Trust, I have intentionally omitted to provide for any of my heirs, or persons claiming to be my heirs, whether or not known to me.

* END OF ARTICLE *

7.

ARTICLE VII

OFFICE OF GUARDIAN

7.1. Nomination of Guardian of the Person.

I nominate HOWARD STERN as guardian and successor guardian of the person of my minor child DANIEL WAYNE SMITH:

Any such nominee who is a resident of a state other than California may, at the nominee's election, file a petition for appointment in such other state and/or in California. I request that any court having jurisdiction permit the guardian to change

WILL OF VICKIE LYNN MARSHALL
-13-

VLM

Attachment 4c(2)
Petition for Probate

Exhibit 5.1 Excerpt from the Will of Anna Nicole Smith

Source: Anna Nicole Smith, Will dated July 30, 2001, proved May 14, 2007, Case Number BP 104574, Superior Court of California, County of Los Angeles, Los Angeles, CA.

the residence and domicile of my minor children to the jurisdiction where the guardian resides.

I give the guardian of the person of my minor children the same authority as a parent having legal custody and authorize the guardian to exercise such authority without need for notice, hearing, court authorization, instructions, approval or confirmation in the same manner as a parent having legal custody. I request that no bond be required because of the grant of these independent powers

7.2. Waiver of Bond.

I request that no bond be required of any guardian nominated above.

* END OF ARTICLES *

Signature Clause. I subscribe my name to this Will at Los Angeles, California, on this ___30th___ day of ___July_____, 2001.

Vickie Lynn Marshall
VICKIE LYNN MARSHALL

Exhibit 5.1 (Continued)

and successor guardian in his client girlfriend's Will. In that case, the legal rights of the natural father prevailed, and the scientific and legal systems worked effectively together.

In situations involving divorced couples, it is not uncommon for one of the child's parents to want someone other than his or her former spouse to be named as the guardian of their minor children. I explain to my clients that a biological parent does not lose his or her fundamental legal rights to raise his or her child, unless there is a serious problem. In America, our family and surrogate's courts have jurisdiction over minor children, and are empowered to do what is in the best interests of the children. On rare occasions, a court will award custody of a minor child to someone other than the natural parent, but the court needs a really good reason to do so. Sometimes, a former spouse is so concerned that she instructs me to include rather strong language in his or her Will advising the world why the former spouse is not fit to be a guardian of their minor children. Such a statement may or may not affect a judge's view of the matter in the future. In some cases, it might be advisable to include such blunt statements about the problems of a former spouse, but beware of libeling another person in your Will, if you decide that you must do so.

Dare I say that father usually knows best? It is a mistake to attempt to deprive the biological parent of his right to be the guardian of his minor children, unless there is a really good reason to do so. Anna Nicole's suited suitor, Howard Stern, was not able to convince a court that Dannielynn's real papa(razzi), Larry Birkhead, should lose his natural parental rights.

Mistake #41: Naming the Biological Parent as the Guardian of Your Minor Children

Now that we have resolved the Anna Nicole custody debacle, let's move on to the more obvious situation of whether or not you should explicitly name your child's biological parent as his or her guardian in your Will. Because the law and the Courts would normally and uniformly appoint the natural parent as the Guardian of your minor child, if it were disputed, it is not usually necessary to state in your Will that the minor child's parent is his or her legal guardian. However, in some instances, it may be a mistake to name the biological parent as the guardian of your minor child.

In his unusually short four-page Last Will and Testament, John Lennon named his wife Yoko Ono as the guardian of their son Sean. It was not necessary for Lennon to name Yoko, the biological parent of Sean, as the legal guardian of Sean's person while he is a minor, because the natural, biological parent is assumed to be the guardian of the person of his or her minor (i.e., under the age of 18) children.

The page of Lennon's Will, which reveals a typographical error in the section that names Lennon's wife Yoko as the "gurdian" [sic] of their son, is reproduced in Exhibit 5.2. (It is also interesting to note that Lennon initialed both the lower right and left side of each page of his short Will.)

As the laws of any state provides that, absent highly unusual circumstances, the biological parent is the guardian of his or her minor offspring until the child reaches the age of 18, it is an unnecessary mistake to name the parent as the guardian, or "gurdian," as the great musician and songwriter John Lennon did in his Will. However, in view of Lennon's untimely death from a deranged fan's bullet in 1980, and his younger son Sean's having become an adult many years ago, we will just have to "let it be."

that I shall have predeceased her and that this, my Will, and any and all of its provisions shall be construed based upon that assumption.

FIFTH: I hereby nominate, constitute and appoint my beloved wife YOKO ONO, to act as the Executor of this my Last Will and Testament. In the event that my beloved wife YOKO ONO shall predecease me or chooses not to act for any reason, I nominate and appoint ELI GARBER, DAVID WARMFLASH and CHARLES PETTIT, in the order named, to act in her place and stead.

SIXTH: I nominate, constitute and appoint my wife YOKO ONO, as the Gurdian of the person and property of any children of the marriage who may survive me. In the event that she predeceases me, or for any reason she chooses not to act in that capacity, I nominate, constitute and appoint SAM GREEN to act in her place and stead.

SEVENTH: No person named herein to serve in any fiduciary capacity shall be required to file or post any bond for the faithful performance of his or her duties, in that capacity in this or in any other jurisdiction, any law to the contrary notwithstanding.

-3-

Exhibit 5.2 Excerpt from the Will of John Lennon
Source: John Lennon, Will dated November 18, 1979, File Number 1980-5773, Surrogate's Court, New York County, New York, NY.

Mistake #42: **Failing To Periodically Review Your Choice of Guardian(s)**

For many people, choosing the guardian of their minor children is the single most important and difficult decision that they need to make in their Wills. It is often a stumbling block and the reason that people often postpone signing their Wills—because they cannot decide or agree with their spouse on who should be named the Guardian of their children while they are under the age of 18 and still considered a minor under federal and state laws. There are so many considerations in that important decision, and I often point out to our clients that there will never be a "perfect" choice, because no one will ever raise your children in exactly the same fashion and manner as you.

Despite the difficulty of choosing the perfect guardian should you and your spouse no longer be around, it is a choice that needs to be made nonetheless. The decision and discussion should involve a thorough consideration of all of the qualified family members or close friends, their relative ages, their health, the perceived stability of their marriages, and their geographical proximity. Depending upon the age of the child, the geographic proximity may be more or less important. For example, a newborn baby would not know the difference between Park Avenue in New York City and Peoria, Illinois, but a teenager would. As the child grows into adolescence, it is probably not a good idea to name guardians who live far from your child's friends.

I also suggest that our clients review their choice of guardian every few years, as it may happen that the perfect couple that you had named as guardians are now going through a nasty divorce. Stuff happens in life, and as this is the single most important decision that you might make for your child, it bears thoughtful consideration and regular reconsideration.

Stuff certainly happened to *West Side Story* actress Natalie Wood during her remarkable lifetime. Wood's life ended in 1981, when she tragically and accidentally drowned to death at the young age of 43 after exiting stage left off her 55-foot yacht, where she had been sailing with her husband, Robert Wagner, and actor Christopher Walken.

Wood's 1980 Will makes it evident how important the decisions about the choice of guardian for her minor children were to Wood. Her Will includes an unusually detailed direction regarding guardianship. Specifically, Wood made it very clear that she wanted to have her two daughters from two different fathers raised together in the same home.[1]

Mistake #43: Assuming That Your Step-Children Have the Same Legal Rights as Your Biological Children

In the multiple-marriage, *Brady Bunch* society that runs rampant throughout the United States, it is not uncommon for a parent to lose sight of his or her various children's or grandchildren's legal rights. It is quite common to find families with children who are adopted, nonmarital, illegitimate, or whatever you would like to call them. Sometimes, parents might even prefer the so-called illegitimate ones to the ones born during an unhappy marriage. But one must understand that the law does make distinctions based on the exact relationship a parent has with their child. The child of your second wife, whom you never officially adopted, does *not* have the same legal rights as the children that you may have sired, and it is a mistake for you to lose sight of that fact.

A big fancy New York law firm failed to point out to its celebrity client that when his Will stated "per stirpes [a Latin term meaning "by the roots" which directs that an estate be divided by the number of families at the first-generational level below the person leaving the property] to my descendants," that his "descendants" did *not* include his former wife's child from her prior marriage, Although this celebrity father felt the same about his step-child as his other biological children, he didn't realize that his Will as written did not provide for her equally as though she were one of his natural children.

One of the reasons that I had the honor of becoming an attorney for this celebrity client, my own "Mr. Big," was because I did my homework. After I received that first telephone call from Mr. Big to schedule our initial meeting, I immediately purchased his recent autobiography and read it cover to cover, with particular attention to his marital history and family relationships. I quickly learned from his book who was who in his family, and I was well-prepared for our first professional meeting, including providing a fine cigar on my desk ready to be smoked if Mr. Big wanted to do so. (He did not, but took the cigar with him.)

I confidently pointed out to Mr. Big that the term "descendants" in his Will should have been defined to include this "daughter" of his who was not, legally, one of his descendants. In the Wills that my law firm prepared for Mr. and Mrs. Big, we clarified their intentions about all of their children, and also improved many other aspects of their Wills.

It is a big mistake not to understand that the term "descendants" or "issue" normally applies to your natural or adopted children, grandchildren, and great-grandchildren, but no one else. It is also a mistake for an attorney preparing a client's Will not to attempt to clarify, record, and reflect accurately in the relevant legal documents all of the client's familial relationships.

Notes

1. Natalie Wood, Will Dated April 17, 1980, proved December 29, 1981, Case Number 669545, Superior Court of California, County of Los Angeles, Los Angeles, CA.

CHAPTER 6

Mistakes Involving Prior Marriages, Prenuptial Agreements, and Significant Others

Playwright William Congreve had it right when he said that Hell hath no fury like a woman scorned. Yet, in our litigious society, this saying is also true for any scorned man, child, or significant other. Unfortunately, there generally is never a shortage of aggrieved parties who are eager to commence a lawsuit if they believe that their spousal or other rights are being affected in a negative way.

In this chapter, I will expose the many estate planning mistakes involving prior marriages, prenuptial agreements, and significant others. The many celebrity mistakes illustrated here show why marriage, divorce, and parenthood are inextricably intertwined with estate planning.

Mistake #44: Not Taking into Account the Terms of an Existing Separation or Divorce Agreement

In an age and society where divorce is commonplace, there will always be a paper trail that memorializes the terms of the dissolution of the marriage. The estate planning attorney needs to be sure that he or she is aware of and has reviewed the terms of any and all existing divorce agreements.

Surprisingly, a prominent national law firm once made the mistake of not reviewing the existing divorce agreement that its client had previously signed. I was retained by the attorneys for the decedent's widow as an expert to provide my opinion as to whether the big firm had been negligent in its preparation of a Last Will and Testament for their deceased client.

The facts are as follows: The extremely wealthy client, who had been divorced, retained the big law firm to prepare his Last Will and Testament. Although the big law firm knew that the client had been divorced, they did not review or apparently ask to review the terms of his final divorce agreement. (This document is often referred to as a "separation agreement," which has been incorporated by reference into a final divorce decree signed by the judge. We will refer to it as the Agreement.)

That Agreement provided that Mr. Wealthy leave at least one-half of his estate, as the term "estate" was defined in the Agreement, to his son from his first marriage. In the case of a very wealthy person, this unusual clause has significant estate tax consequences because the portion of the estate that is in excess of the available exemption amount and is not passing to the surviving spouse or to a tax-exempt charity would be subject to estate tax.

Because of this Agreement, it really did not matter what Mr. Wealthy's Will said in regard to dividing his estate. He and his estate had a legal obligation to pay one-half of the very large estate to his son. That resulted in substantial state and federal estate taxes, all of which Mr. Wealthy's widow had to pay, including the taxable portion passing to her step-son. She was not amused, and she was rightfully angry with her attorneys who were allegedly aware of the existence of the Agreement but did not take it into account in their preparation of the decedent's Will.

Although the big law firm might have been negligent in its handling of the decedent's Will and estate planning, they had the protections of *privity* and lack of damages to shield them from liability. As they had no legal relationship, or *privity*, with the decedent's widow, they had no legal duty toward her. Their obligation was to their deceased client. As a result, they could always take the unassailable position that the terms of the Will were what their client wanted and told them to do, after of course they had explained all of the ramifications of his choice to him. It was also true that the widow who went berserk over this situation was able to settle the claim of her step-son for a fraction of its true value, and she ended up with much more of the estate than she expected. She would have been hard pressed to show that she had been damaged as a result of the law firm's activities. In fact, she exited this scenario as a very wealthy woman, and was rumored to be "hooking up" with that law firm's senior partner.

As evidenced by this story, it was a big mistake for the fancy law firm not to review the terms of their client's divorce Agreement and to reflect those terms in their client's estate planning. At my first meeting with a new client, I always ask about the existence of any divorce or separation agreements, and if there are any, I always ask the client to provide us with a copy of the duly executed original Agreement. This mistake can easily be avoided if the proper questions are asked by the attorney preparing the estate plan, and by you, the client, bringing a copy of any existing divorce agreements that would affect your estate planning options.

Mistake #45: Entirely Disinheriting Children or Grandchildren Out of Stupidity or Inadvertence

Although we can point to numerous examples of people who have expressly disinherited their children or grandchildren out of anger or vindictiveness (see Mistake #68), it is less common to see a descendant be disinherited inadvertently or out of carelessness or stupidity. But it happens.

Anna Nicole Smith (AKA Vickie Lynn Marshall), whom we already mentioned in connection with Mistake #40, signed her Last Will and Testament on July 30, 2001. In February of 2007, just a short six years later, she was found dead in a hotel room at the Hard Rock Hotel and Casino in Hollywood, Florida. At the age of 39, Anna Nicole had only one legal heir: her six-month-old daughter Dannielynn. Three days after the birth of her daughter, Ms. Smith had lost her 20-year-old son Daniel, when he allegedly died of a drug overdose in the same hospital in the Bahamas in which his mother had just given birth to his baby sister Dannielynn.

The first page of the Will of Vickie Lynn Marshal, shown in Exhibit 6.1, shows Anna Nicole's unequivocal and rather unusual statement that she has "intentionally omitted to provide for my spouse and other heirs, including future spouses and children and other descendants now living and those hereafter born or adopted, as well as existing and future stepchildren and foster children."[1]

What were Anna Nicole Smith and her attorneys thinking? Why would a mother ever expressly disinherit any and all of her future children? As Anna Nicole Smith's tragic final year unfolded, her son Daniel died six months before his mother, and three days after the

indirectly, contests or attacks this Will or the Trust or any of the provisions of said instruments, or conspires with or assists anyone in any such contest, or pursues any creditor's claim that my Executor reasonably deems to constitute a contest, any share or interest in my estate or the Trust given to that contesting beneficiary under this Will or the Trust is revoked and shall be disposed of as if the contesting beneficiary had predeceased me without descendants, and shall augment proportionately the shares of my estate passing to or in trust for my beneficiaries who have not participated in such acts. This Article shall not apply to a disclaimer. Expenses to resist a contest or other attack of any nature shall be paid from my estate as expenses of administration.

6.2. General Disinheritance.

Except as otherwise provided herein and in the Trust, I have intentionally omitted to provide for any of my heirs, or persons claiming to be my heirs, whether or not known to me.

* END OF ARTICLE *

7.   ARTICLE VII
                OFFICE OF GUARDIAN

7.1. Nomination of Guardian of the Person.

I nominate HOWARD STERN as guardian and successor guardian of the person of my minor child DANIEL WAYNE SMITH:

Any such nominee who is a resident of a state other than California may, at the nominee's election, file a petition for appointment in such other state and/or in California. I request that any court having jurisdiction permit the guardian to change

WILL OF VICKIE LYNN MARSHALL
-13-

VLM
VLM

Attachment 4c(2)
Petition for Probate

Exhibit 6.1 Excerpt from the Will of Anna Nicole Smith

Source: Anna Nicole Smith, Will dated July 30, 2001, proved May 14, 2007, Case Number BP 104574, Superior Court of California, County of Los Angeles, Los Angeles, CA.

birth of his baby sister Dannielynn. Is there any reason to believe that Anna Nicole Smith did not intend to treat her daughter the same way as she had intended to treat her son?

The problem is probably more with the legal document itself than with Ms. Smith, as it is hard to imagine that she would have made the effort to analyze the terms of a boring legal document that was prepared by her lawyers and trusted advisors.

Based on the foregoing, it is clear that Howard Stern was Anna Nicole's top legal eagle in 2001, but although they never quite made it to the marital altar (and thereby totally undermined his legal rights). He was still with her at the Hard Rock Hotel on the day she died. Hard luck at the Hard Rock.

The obvious problem with the Will of Anna Nicole Smith is probably more an example of mediocre legal work than Anna Nicole's malicious desire to disinherit her own child. In the six months that she spent with her daughter Dannielynn, it was evident that a strong mother-daughter relationship was developing between them. After the death or her son Daniel, one would have assumed that the attorneys involved in the preparation of Anna Nicole's Will would have pointed out to her that the Will did not provide for any other beneficiaries. Hence, her poorly drafted Will was never changed before the tragic end of her life.

Be sure that your Will makes sense. If it does not make sense to you when you read it, it is a mistake not to ask your attorney to explain it to you in a satisfactory manner.

Mistake #46: Not Taking Your Spouse's Legal or Statutory Rights into Account

The laws of every state in the United States protect the rights of a spouse to inherit from the estate of the other spouse, regardless of the terms of any Will or testamentary substitute that the other spouse may have, in the absence of a valid prenuptial agreement. This is often called the spouse's *right of election.* Simply put, this right entitles one to a certain percentage or fraction of the estate of one's spouse. In many states, this amount may be one-third of the value of one's spouse's estate. This fraction must be paid outright to the electing spouse, and a trust holding that fractional amount for the decedent spouse does not usually satisfy the spouse's statutory right of election.

To assert the right of election, certain legal steps need to be taken within a certain time frame. However, the right of election is provided and protected by the laws and statutes of the various states. Those laws should be carefully reviewed to ensure that the proper legal steps are effectuated in a timely manner.

It is a mistake to have an estate plan that does not take your spouse's statutory rights into account. Even if your Will states otherwise, your spouse's statutory rights apply. Even the inclusion of a no contest clause in your Will does not defeat your spouse's legal rights. If you don't take those rights into account while doing your estate planning, your entire estate plan could be thwarted and undermined by your spouse's exercise of his or her legal rights.

Mistake #47: Putting Your Child in Charge of a Surviving Spouse Who Is Not His or Her Parent

One of the most difficult decisions many people face when preparing their Wills is determining who would be best suited to serve as the fiduciary in charge of administering their estates. This decision becomes even more difficult when the testator or testatrix is married and has children from a prior marriage or relationship. In most instances, it would be prudent for a testator to choose the most capable individual. However, Mistake #47 demonstrates that it is a bad idea to put your child in charge of a surviving spouse who is not his or her parent. Thus, it may be best in situations where the testator is married and has children from a prior relationship to choose a fiduciary from his extended family, or a qualified fiduciary with no familial ties at all.

A prime example of why a testator or testatrix should not place children from a prior marriage in a position of authority over his or her surviving spouse involves the estate of Vincente Minnelli, the famed director of musicals and father of singer/actress Liza Minnelli. Under article eighth of his Last Will and Testament, Mr. Minnelli appointed his daughter Liza as his Executor. In addition, under article fifth of the Will, Mr. Minnelli bequeathed his Beverley Hills home to his daughter Liza, and granted his wife the right to reside in the home, or, if Liza chose to sell the property, a "suitable apartment or other place of residence."[2]

As one might imagine, explicitly granting Liza the authority to sell the residence occupied by her stepmother created problems, and that appointment may have been a casting mistake by director Minnelli.

When selecting a trustee for your surviving spouse, it is a mistake not to think long and hard about the relationship between your spouse and your trustee. More than likely, this relationship will undoubtedly change after your death. Don't let your estate plan suffer from that change in relationship status.

Mistake #48: Assuming That Your Divorce Automatically Revokes Your Will in Its Entirety

In view of the high rate of divorce throughout the United States, it would make sense for each state's probate and estate laws to provide that some part, or all, of your Will is automatically and legally revoked as soon as your divorce from your spouse becomes final. The practical reality behind the law may be that a person is too preoccupied on the dissolution of his marriage to have the desire or the energy or the money to also simultaneously focus on changing his own estate planning documents to take into account that his former spouse is now an "ex." It could also be that your matrimonial lawyer is so expensive that there is nothing left to pay your estate planning attorney. But beware of assuming that your divorce necessarily revokes your *entire* Will, and not just the parts of the Will that apply only to your ex-wife or -husband.

I handled the estate of an attorney who was divorced from his attorney wife, but had never changed his Will after their divorce. Although the sections of his Will that provided for his wife were automatically revoked by operation of law, and his entire estate passed to their three children, there was still a problem. Although the decedent's ex-wife could not act as the named executor, *her* best friend had been named as the successor executor. That successor executor, who was also an attorney, often consulted with her close friend, the decedent's ex-wife. As a result, the ex-wife was involved with her ex-husband's estate every single step of the way. Whether the decedent would have been concerned or troubled by that situation we will never know.

The lesson from this mistake is rather simple—be sure to check into the laws of your state regarding the impact of your divorce on your Will. Also, review any other estate planning–related documents, such as a general or limited power of attorney or living will/healthcare proxy. It is a mistake to assume that your recent or even long ago divorce automatically revokes all of the terms of your Will.

Mistake #49: Not Updating Your Will at the Start of Your Divorce Proceedings

The sad reality is that divorces take a long time to conclude, and it may not be advisable to wait to let the finality of the divorce revoke the terms of the Will for your hoped-to-be ex-spouse. Wall Street financier Ted Ammon definitely had the money to pay his estate planning attorneys at one of New York's fanciest and most expensive firms, but as a "Master of the Universe," he may have believed that he would never die. Unfortunately, he died soon and in a very ugly way: He was found bludgeoned to death in the bedroom of his very fancy East Hampton home in 2001, and his then-wife's boyfriend, Danny Pelosi, was convicted of his murder. If Mr. Pelosi knew that Ted Ammon had never updated his Will, which provided very generously for Ammon's estranged wife Generosa, then it could be fairly said that Ted Ammon may have died because he failed to update his Will while going through a very bitter and expensive divorce.

For a variety of reasons, it is a mistake not to at least review and update your Will at the start of your separation or divorce proceedings. I urge clients to change or entirely eliminate the provisions for their future ex-spouses as soon as possible in the divorce process. First, it may make you feel better knowing that you have been able to unilaterally make an important decision without having to negotiate with your spouse's matrimonial attorney. Second, depending on what is going on in your life, you want to be sure that your soon-to-be-ex-spouse will not have easy access to your address book or your "dirty laundry," if you were to die before your divorce was final. Finally, not attending to updating your estate planning documents in a timely manner could possibly lead to your untimely demise, as Ted Ammon found out the hard way.

So, as soon as the separation or divorce proceedings begin, run—don't walk—to your divorce *and* estate planning attorney and begin making those changes to your Will.

Mistake #50: Not Respecting the Validity of a Prenuptial Agreement

If you signed a prenuptial agreement prior to your wedding, and there was full disclosure of assets and liabilities, and each side was represented by competent counsel, it is a mistake not to accept the fact that that agreement will be upheld if it is ever questioned in the context of the estate of one of the signatories to that agreement. Like most contracts, it will be upheld by a court that is asked to opine as to its validity.

When we are asked to prepare a prenuptial agreement for a client, we try to complete it as soon as possible for everyone's benefit, and certainly before the wedding invitations have been sent out. Unfortunately, the message does not always get through to both parties, who may begin to believe that an ante-nuptial agreement is more about being anti-nuptial.

There are often many good reasons for people who are getting married to have a written understanding of their respective rights as to the property of the other. A written agreement about the disposition of that property upon one spouse's subsequent death, or upon divorce if that should happen, can often avoid expense and aggravation later. But if you want a signed agreement, then you need to give yourself plenty of lead time before the six-weeks-until-the-wedding date, when the wedding invitations are sent out, and your marital plans are announced, and your negotiating leverage is greatly diminished.

Mistake #51: Not Mentioning the Prenuptial Agreement in Your Will

Unfortunately, some people out there just do not like their spouses anymore. They have grown apart and no longer like even being around each other. Sometimes the relationship has turned into true malice, and these unhappily married people do not want to provide more than they have to for their spouses when they die. It is their ultimate revenge, and the last power play, to give their spouses as little as possible after they are gone.

Yet a problem may arise if the Will gives the spouse less than the state law provides that a spouse is entitled to receive. In every state, spouses have important legal rights and interests in the property of their spouse, upon his or her death, unless they have made some agreement to the contrary, either as an existing prenuptial agreement or as a postnuptial agreement.

If you are providing for your spouse at an amount less than what state law provides, based on the terms of a written prenuptial agreement with your spouse, it would be a mistake not to refer to that agreement in your Will. By referring to the agreement in the Will, the attorney not only must review its terms and draft the Will accordingly, but the reference to the existence of the agreement will minimize the likelihood of a legal dispute over the existence and terms of such an agreement when the Will is being probated in the future.

Mistake #52: Failing to Fund a Revocable Living Trust During Your Lifetime to Avoid Probate

Many people have been advised that they can avoid probate if they establish a revocable or living or *inter vivos* trust during their lifetime. Merely establishing that trust is not enough to avoid probate, however, and many people fall into the following trust trap, which I recently helped one of my most intelligent and financially and personally successful clients avoid. Fortunately, he was smart enough to recently engage us as his attorneys and to take our advice.

Many people ask me whether a revocable living trust is a good substitute for a Will because it supposedly avoids probate. I explain that such a trust would avoid the need to probate, or prove, a person's Last Will and Testament only *if* all of that person's assets have been transferred during his lifetime into the name of the trust, so that there would be no assets in the decedent's name individually that would pass pursuant to his Will.

My new, smart, savvy client first showed me the trust agreement that had been prepared by the fancy law firm that was our predecessor as his attorneys. I asked my client if all of the assets had been transferred into the name of the trust. He told me that not a single asset had been transferred. I then explained that even though his Will had been structured as a so-called *pour over* Will, his Will would need to be probated because all of his assets were still in his name, and there would have to be a court proceeding to accomplish that. My new client told me that his prior lawyer had never told him that he needed to transfer the assets into the name of the trust that had been established. What my new client might have said to his former lawyer about the failure to advise him properly about transferring his assets into the name of the trust, I do not know, but I do not think it was too pretty.

Any lawyer who establishes a living trust for a client for the purpose of avoiding probate and does not advise the client to transfer the assets into the name of that trust during his lifetime is making a mistake. In this particular case, the prior lawyers' mistake was my gain, as I was able to land an important new client as a result of the oversight, and dare I say, negligence, of the attorneys who preceded me in this matter.

If you really want to avoid probate, then you need to be sure to transfer all of your assets into your living trust during your lifetime, or hold your assets as a joint tenant with a right of survivorship and be sure that you die before your co-owner does. It is a big mistake to assume that merely establishing a trust during your lifetime will avoid probate if you have not addressed the question of the title on all of your assets. In short, watch your assets.

Notes

1. Anna Nicole Smith, Will dated July 30, 2001, proved May 14, 2007, Case Number BP 104574, Superior Court of California, County of Los Angeles, Los Angeles, CA.
2. Vincente Minelli, Will dated June 23, 1983, proved August 9, 1988, Case Number P 709359, Superior Court of California, County of Los Angeles, Los Angeles, CA.

Estate Planning Mistakes Involving Tax and Copyright Issues

Ben Franklin had it only partially right when he said that "nothing can said to be certain, except death and taxes."

There are ways around taxes that allow you to avoid, but not evade, paying them. For people with very large estates, the implications of a simple mistake could result in millions if not billions of dollars in unnecessary estate taxes. There are many traps for the unwary, and it is a mistake not to consult with experienced estate tax counsel when making estate planning decisions. At a combined federal and state estate tax rate of approximately 50 percent, a mistake in your planning could be devastating to your family and their pocketbooks. In this chapter, I outline eight estate planning mistakes as they pertain to issues surrounding taxes and copyrights.

Mistake #53: Eliminating Your Residuary Estate Because of High Taxes on Your Personal Property

The calculation of the estate tax starts with the addition of all the property that you own on the date of your death. This calculation is often referred to as your *gross estate*. From this sum, various deductions, including the unlimited marital and charitable deductions, are subtracted. Based on that arithmetic and some other, more complicated, calculations, the value of your *taxable estate* is determined.

Mistake #53 occurs when you fail to recognize that estate taxes attributable to your tangible personal property could eliminate your residuary estate. In other words, if the tangible personal property that you owned nets more than $35 million in sale proceeds, and that amount is paid to your surviving children, and there is no applicable marital or charitable deduction, there will be a large amount of estate tax due. That estate tax on just your tangible personal property could wipe out your residuary estate and thwart your estate plan. This is the problem that faced the estate of Jacqueline Kennedy Onassis, who died in 1994 at the age of 64.

Jackie O's Will, which was signed two months before she died, contemplated a charitable lead annuity trust (CLAT) to be comprised of her residuary estate.[1] The charity, which was intended to receive the income from that lead trust for 24 years, was to be called The C&J Foundation (a name derived from the first initials of her two children's names). The remainder of the estate was to pass to Jackie's grandchildren or other descendants living in the year 2018. If no descendants of John F. Kennedy, Jr. or Caroline Kennedy Schlossberg were then living, the remainder was directed

---

to pass one-half to the living descendants of Jackie's cousin, Michel Bouvier, and one-half to the living descendants of her sister Lee B. Radziwill, or the entire amount to either if no descendants of the other survived.

The trustees of the C&J Foundation—Caroline, John, attorney Forger, and boyfriend Tempelsman—were directed to pay the income to qualified charitable organizations of their choice. However, the Will also included Jackie's "wish" that "in selecting the particular qualified charitable beneficiaries which shall be the recipients of benefits from the Foundation the independent Trustees give preferential consideration to such eligible organization or organizations the purposes and endeavors of which the independent *Trustees feel are committed to making a significant difference in the cultural or social betterment of mankind or the relief of human suffering.*" (emphasis added)

Unfortunately, the best-laid charitable plans went astray in this case, as there was no residuary estate remaining after the taxes and expenses were paid to fund that charitable trust or to establish the C&J Foundation. It was a mistake for Jackie O's super-fancy law firm to lose sight of the fact that the estate taxes on their client's pre-residuary bequests would wipe out her residuary estate and lead to an ineffective estate plan.

Mistake #54: Not Taking Full Advantage of the Available Tax Exemption Amount

Current U.S. and state estate tax laws provide for an exempt amount that can pass free of estate tax. The federal exemption amount is currently $3.5 million. Although President Obama has publicly stated his administration's desire to maintain that exemption amount level in future years, Congress can change the terms of the estate tax laws whenever it wants, and it often does. In addition, every single state's tax laws specify a certain amount of property that can pass free of estate tax after your death. For instance, the New York exemption amount is currently $1 million; Connecticut's is $2 million; and New Jersey's is $675,000. For larger estates with millions of dollars in assets, it is advisable to structure your estate plan so that you do not lose part or all of the available exemption amount. Use it or lose it

For example, let's say that you leave your entire hypothetical $10 million estate to your husband or wife. As that gift to your spouse would qualify for the current unlimited marital deduction, there would be no estate tax. However, the tax problem arises when your surviving spouse dies, and his or her estate may now be $2 million or $3.5 million larger than it had to be because you did not use the exemption amount available to your estate. Your surviving spouse's estate will be subject to unnecessary and significant estate taxes that could have been avoided through proper planning.

To avoid this estate planning mistake, I urge you to create a so-called by-pass trust, which would be available for the use of your spouse during his or her lifetime but would pass to your children, or anyone else you wanted, upon the death of your spouse. The by-pass trust would not be included in your spouse's estate, and the applicable estate taxes would be avoided. As this is a very standard estate planning technique, it would be a mistake not to use it, especially if you have an estate with substantial assets.

So much has been said about Leona Helmsley's Will in this book and the media that I figured we should take a moment to give equal time to Leona's husband, Harry. We could all agree that Harry Helmsley died with a substantial estate worth hundreds of millions of dollars, if not billions, when he died in 1997. Despite his enormous wealth, Helmsley's Will made a single $25,000 bequest to his longtime secretary Ceil Fried; the rest was left to his queen.[2] There were two other bequests to individuals in Harry's 1994 Will, but those were conditional upon the queen not surviving the king. As we know, Leona Helmsley hung on to her throne 10 years longer, until she died in 2007. If Harry Helmsley did not make substantial lifetime gifts which used up his exemption amount, he made a mistake by not making larger bequests under his Will. However, because Leona left her estate to a charitable foundation with a mission to protect and care for dogs, there would not have been any additional estate tax due from her estate, so maybe Harry had it right all along. Whether his longtime secretary was satisfied with a $25,000 bequest we will never know.

If you can afford to do so, it is a mistake not to structure your estate plan to take advantage of all or part of the federal or state estate tax exemption amount available to your estate.

Mistake #55: Not Having Assets Titled in the Name of Each Spouse

After reading the previous Mistake, you should now understand that if you do not use it ("it" being the estate tax exemption amount), you lose it. With this understanding, you and your spouse may have carefully selected a top attorney who charges you a top price to carefully prepare and draft your Wills. Now, you think your Wills will be perfect. But I caution you—they probably are not perfect. In fact, the problem could be that the title to your assets is not coordinated with your estate plan.

What does this mean? As an example, if all of your assets are jointly held by you and your spouse, and not in your name individually, there will be no assets available in your estate to fund the by-pass trust or other bequests under your Will. As a result of this poor estate planning, you may fall victim to Mistake #55—not having assets titled in the name of each spouse to individually use part or all of the available exemption amount. Thus, your estate planning may be undermined, and significant and unnecessary additional estate taxes may be due and payable.

It is a common and costly mistake not to review the title on your assets at the same time that your Wills or trusts are being prepared. When reviewing these documents, be sure that the titles are coordinated with the legal documents and you have an effective estate plan in place. If your assets are not titled properly, the best laid estate plans will definitely "gang aft agley," as the poet Robert Burns once wrote. It is a mistake not to look at the big estate planning picture involving the exact title on your assets as well as the terms of your legal documents.

Mistake #56: Failing to Ascertain Whether Gift Tax Returns Were Ever Filed

The federal estate and gift tax system is often referred to as a unified tax system because the estate taxes payable can be affected by large gifts that may have been made during the decedent's lifetime. The federal government will tax a person on lifetime gifts in excess of $1 million, excluding annual exclusion gifts (currently $13,000 per donee per donor per year).

A problem arises when the person who is preparing and filing the federal and state estate tax returns is not aware of the taxable gifts made by the decedent. If those gifts were substantial and used some or all of the decedent's lifetime exemption, then the estate tax will be higher than expected, and that could cause trouble for the executor and/or the beneficiaries. The failure to include gift tax returns that have been filed with the Internal Revenue Service (IRS) could also lead to the selection of that light estate tax return for an audit.

How do you avoid this estate planning mistake? First, you should check with the decedent's accountant, spouse, or other close relatives to determine whether gift tax returns were ever filed (for lifetime gifts exceeding the federal annual exclusion amount, which is now pegged at $13,000 per calendar year.) If they say "no" or "nothing" but the executor has reason to suspect that gifts may have been made, the executor may ask the IRS to check its records as to whether it shows the filing of any gift tax returns (Form 709). If it does, those returns can be ordered from the IRS for a small fee. But do not delay in looking into the question of lifetime gifts, as it may take a few months or more to assemble all of the relevant records.

It is a mistake not to determine whether gift tax returns were ever filed by the decedent. If they were, be sure to factor those gifts into the calculation of the estate taxes that are payable from the estate. However, if you fail to ascertain whether gift tax returns were ever filed or, for that matter, whether significant taxable gifts were made by the decedent during his lifetime, there could be unpleasant news from the IRS, including additional estates taxes, plus interest and/or penalties.

Mistake #57: Failing to Pay the Five Percent Annual Minimum Distribution Requirement for Private Charitable Foundations

One of life's most rewarding experiences is to be able to make a real difference in one's community through charitable giving. Many individuals have experienced that kind of reward by creating a private charitable foundation. However, for many well-intentioned donors, founders, and directors of these private foundations, they often fall into common mistakes in administering a private foundation. Fortunately, you may now avoid making one important estate planning mistake—failing to pay the five percent annual minimum distribution requirement.

The IRS requires that all private foundations distribute an amount equal to five percent of the value of the foundation's net investment assets on an annual basis. Essentially, a foundation with $1 million in assets in 2008 must make at least $50,000 of qualifying distributions by the end of 2009. However, many foundations fail to make the required minimum five percent distribution by the *end of the year*.

The consequences of failing to meet the payout requirement are quite expensive. A foundation that does not distribute the required amount by the deadline is subject to an initial penalty equal to 30 percent of the deficient amount. The foundation is required to distribute that deficient amount or be accountable to a penalty equal to *200 percent* of the deficient amount. Using our example above of a foundation with $1 million in assets, the worst case scenario could translate into a penalty of more than $100,000. At this point, you may be wondering what distributions count toward the five percent payout requirement. A private foundation may count any administrative expenses that are necessary and *reasonable* for the foundation to conduct its charitable activities. Reasonable administrative expenses may include the following:

- Executive, board and staff compensation, training/professional development
- Professional, legal, and accounting fees
- Office supplies, telephone charges, publishing the foundation's annual report
- Modest travel expenses associated with the foundation's business
- Any similar activities and costs incurred to carry out the foundation's charitable mission

These costs, along with grants, make up a large part of a private foundation's qualifying distributions that count toward its five percent payout requirement.

However, expenses that cannot be included are investment fees, which include ongoing investment management, consultant fees, attending investment conferences, and custodial fees.

One last interesting rule to remember is that if you have made a distribution beyond the five percent requirement, *excess* distributions may be carried forward for up to five years to meet future distribution requirements. In other words, if you feel particularly generous this year, that generosity may be applied toward your future distribution requirements; however, the excess distributions may not be carried back to satisfy under distributions from previous years. So, be sure to coordinate with your accountant to be sure that your charitable distributions meet the minimum requirements to avoid any nasty and unnecessary tax penalties that could reduce your estate or your foundation's charitable resources.

Mistake #58: Not Having a Buy-Sell Agreement in a Closely Held Business, Partnership, or Limited Liability Corporation

If you own a closely held business, are a partner in a business, or are a member of a limited liability corporation (LLC), it would be a mistake not to consider adopting a buy-sell agreement. A buy-sell agreement allows an owner, shareholder, or partner to control his/her business' destiny in the event of his/her death, disability, retirement, termination of employment, or bankruptcy. Consider a buy-sell agreement as sort of a "business will" or "prenuptial agreement" between business partners or shareholders. Just as a Will or prenuptial agreement would ensure a stable transition and minimize disputes among family members (in this case, it can be both family members and business owners), having a buy-sell agreement in place can help resolve those same issues and protect and preserve your interest in the business.

A common scenario in which a buy-sell agreement can be a powerful tool is when a large portion of an owner's estate is comprised of his interest in a closely held business. Not having a buy-sell agreement under this scenario will make it difficult for the estate to raise the cash necessary to pay the administration expenses and any tax liabilities. On the other hand, a buy-sell agreement can be drafted so that upon the owner's death, all or part of the owner's interest can be purchased from his estate, ensuring liquidity for the estate. Also, the owner can directly get involved in the price negotiation to ensure that the price payable for his business interest is fair and sufficient, rather than leaving the task to the executor or beneficiaries who may not be familiar with the business.

If you are considering adopting a buy-sell agreement, you should know that there are two main types of buy-sell agreements: redemption agreements and cross-purchase agreements. With a redemption agreement, the corporation itself buys back a shareholder's stock or interest of the departing owner. With a cross-purchase agreement, the remaining owner individually agrees to redeem the business interest of the deceased. There is also an option to use a hybrid of the two agreements. To draft an agreement that satisfies your desired results, you should get the recommendations of both your attorney and accountant.

In a nutshell, buy-sell agreements can save a lot of time and money for yourself and for your beneficiaries, protect an owner's interest in a business, and ensure prudent estate planning. Therefore, I urge any business or LLC owner to have a properly executed buy-sell agreement in place. However, it is a commonly made mistake not to do so.

Mistake #59: Failing to Title Appreciated Real Estate in the Name of the Spouse More Likely to Die First

The current federal estate tax law allows for a stepped-up basis when valuing the assets in a decedent's estate. The stepped-up basis is based on the fair market value of all property owned by the decedent on the date of his or her death, and it replaces the prior cost basis of that same property. Therefore, it is very advantageous from a capital gains tax perspective to have a new increased basis, so that when the estate sells that property, the gain will be minimized or eliminated.

A very genteel and fancy Park Avenue couple, who were close friends of my parents and subsequently became clients of mine, made a mistake involving their valuable Park Avenue apartment, for which the attorney involved (me) was told to accept the blame. You be the judge.

At a certain point in this Park Avenue marriage, the wife found out that her much older husband was having an affair. In an attempt to extract some personal justice, the couple agreed to transfer the ownership of their valuable cooperative apartment from the husband's name into the name of his much-younger wife. Unfortunately, I was not told of this transfer at the time, as they wanted to maintain privacy as to why it was being done. When the husband died several years later, I was finally advised of the transfer of the title to their co-operative apartment. Because the co-operative apartment was now in the name of the younger, surviving spouse, she did not get the benefit of a stepped-up date of death basis, which would have been the case if the apartment had been owned in the name of her deceased husband. When she subsequently sold the apartment, she had to pay a substantial capital gains tax on the difference between the sale price and the cost basis in the apartment that she received when her husband gifted it to her many years earlier.

Should I (or any attorney) have been expected to delve into the title of their assets on an ongoing basis? Was it a mistake for me not to send all of my clients a memo on this issue to avoid this happening to any of them? I don't think so. However, somehow this glamorous widow decided that it was my fault that she had to pay such a high capital gains tax, despite the fact that she had an enormous gain on the sale. Sometimes the lawyer just can't win. So, for all of my clients reading this out there, make sure to have certain highly appreciated assets titled in the name of the spouse most likely to die first, so that you may take optimal advantage of the stepped-up basis rules that are available to minimize capital gains taxes.

Mistake #60: Separating the Copyright Interest from the Actual Work of Art That Is Bequeathed to a Charity

In closing up this chapter on estate planning mistakes as they relate to tax issues, I want to discuss a tax trap that happens to many artists or collectors who separate the copyright interest from the artwork itself. If you intend to bequeath a valuable piece of art to a charity, be sure not to separate the copyright from the painting.

Under federal copyright laws, the copyright in a work of art is considered to be separate and apart from the physical work of art itself. Therefore, if a work of art is donated to a charity or given or sold to an individual, that does not necessarily carry the copyright along with the transfer of the physical object. The copyright law requires that copyrights should be expressly transferred or otherwise pass pursuant to the operation of the applicable estate and copyright laws.

This area of the tax code is complicated, but if you insist on delving into it, you should refer to Sections 170(e)(1)(B)(i), 501(c)(3), 2055(e)(4)(c), and 4942(j)(3) of the Internal Revenue Code. Section 2055(e) provides that the copyright in the work and the art work itself be treated as separate properties. Therefore, if a bequest of an artwork is made to a charitable organization, and the copyright is not also transferred to that charitable organization, it may result in the loss of the charitable deduction that would otherwise be available to the estate.

It is a big mistake not to get the benefit of sophisticated legal advice if some or all of your assets consist of valuable artworks that you are considering bequeathing to a museum or other charitable institution. If you fall victim to Mistake #60, you may inadvertently lose a valuable charitable deduction that would otherwise be available to your estate. To avoid this mistake, I urge you to seek the advice of an estate tax attorney with special expertise in the specific laws that apply to the donation of works of art to charitable institutions.

Notes

1. Jaqueline Kennedy Onassis, Will dated May 15, 1984, proved October 25, 1984, File Number 3100-1985, Surrogate's Court, County of New York, New York, NY.
2. Harry Helmsley, Will dated January 21, 1994, proved January 9, 1996, File Number 1997-0085, Surrogate's Court, County of New York, New York, NY.

8

Estate Planning Mistakes Involving Disgruntled Friends and Family

As bad as things can get with family, things sometimes gets even worse with people who are not your family but want to be treated that way anyway. The mistakes in this chapter run the gamut of human relationships and also highlight the changing cultural mores of the times in which we are living.

From Rock Hudson to Groucho Marx, you might even get a laugh from some of the strange but true things that you are about to read. People often make mistakes in their human relationships. A Will can be used to settle a score or continue to control from the grave. However, the problem with making a mistake in your Will that might take effect after you die is that you can't change it at that point. It is immutable. Therefore, it is advisable to think twice or even three times when making decisions that may have a negative impact on the ones that are closest to you, including your attorney.

Mistake #61: Lack of a No Contest or *In Terrorem* Clause in Your Will

As litigation involving estates seems to be more and more commonplace, it is a mistake not to do everything that you can in your estate planning and in your estate planning documents to avoid litigation. Once you have made the decision that you will be leaving less to a relative than the amount to which he or she would otherwise be entitled (or thinks he or she should be entitled), you have to expect that your decision may cause some kind of dispute after you are gone. One way to attempt to avoid a Will contest is to include a so-called no contest or in terrorem clause in your Will.

You don't need to be a celebrity to benefit from the use of an *in terrorem* (Latin for "in fright" or "in terror") or no contest clause in your Will. An in terrorem clause in a Will threatens the forfeiture of a beneficiary's bequest or interest under the Will should that beneficiary contest the validity of the Will in court and lose. These terrifying clauses should be drawn broadly to apply to anyone who directly or indirectly contests any part or all of the Will.

If a Will contest is foreseen or even foreseeable, it is a mistake not to include a valid no contest clause in your Will in an attempt to avoid the expense and aggravation that would result from a Will contest.

Mistake #62: Using a One-Dollar No Contest/*In Terrorem* Clause in Your Will

As much as it may be a mistake to omit a no contest clause in your Will, it may be an even bigger, but more subtle, mistake to have such a clause in your Will but not to provide a significant bequest to the person being disinherited.

If a person receives something of value under the Will, he will have to consider whether it is worth risking the amount that has been provided in the Will by contesting the Will. Including such a bequest raises the stakes and the ante for embarking on a Will contest, and therefore it may be a mistake not to leave some amount of money to a person who needs to consider whether it is worth losing the amount that he or she is being given.

Despite the foregoing wisdom, the following excerpt in Exhibit 8.1 from the Will of actress Mae West reveals an ineffective no contest clause.

Maybe one dollar used to be a lot of money in America, but I doubt it. It would be a mistake to rely on a one-dollar bequest to attempt to avoid a Will contest today, and it was probably also a mistake in 1964 when West signed her Last Will and Testament. Mae West had reached the very ripe old age of 87 when she died in 1980. The Western strategy may have been to let the Will contest proceed, but then to reward the winner with a one-dollar prize. That may sound like a shrewd strategy, but if the whole Will is knocked out in a Will contest, then the one-dollar bequest goes with it.

Whether you are a celebrity or not, the best way to avoid a Will contest is to determine the legal rights of all of your close relatives and treat them accordingly in your estate planning. Even if you really don't like your spouse or your children, it is a mistake to attempt to cut them out of your estate plan altogether. If you really want to stick it to them, include an enforceable no contest clause in your Will and make a meaningful bequest to that person, causing him or her to think twice before contesting your Will.

1. One-seventh (1/7) to the MOTION PICTURE RELIEF FUND, a charitable organization;

2. One-seventh (1/7) to the CITY OF HOPE, a charitable organization;

3. One-seventh (1/7) to the UNITED CRUSADE, a charitable organization;

4. One-seventh (1/7) to the SALVATION ARMY, a charitable organization;

5. One-seventh (1/7) to the AMERICAN BROTHER-HOOD OF BLIND, a charitable organization;

6. One-seventh (1/7) to the HOLLYWOOD COMEDY CLUB, a charitable organization;

7. One-seventh (1/7) to the CEDARS-SINAI HOSPITAL of LOS ANGELES, CALIFORNIA, a non-profit corporation.

In the event that any bequest or devise herein should be held to be wholly or partially invalid under the provisions of the California Probate Code relating to gifts to charity, then that portion of my estate which the charitable legatee or devisee named herein is prevented from receiving shall go and be distributed in equal shares to the beneficiaries set forth in Sub-paragraph A of this Paragraph Seventh of this Will.

EIGHTH: I have intentionally omitted making provision for all of my heirs who are not specifically mentioned herein, and I hereby generally and specifically disinherit each, any and all persons whomsoever claiming to be or who may law-fully be determined to be my heirs at law, except as such are mentioned in this Will, and if any of such persons, or such heirs, or any devisees, or legatees, or beneficiaries, under this Will shall contest in any court any of the provisions of this instrument, or shall not defend or assist in good faith

Exhibit 8.1 Excerpt from the Will of Mae West

Source: Mae West, Will dated June 3, 1988, proved April 3, 1989, Case Number P 732515, Superior Court of California, County of Los Angeles, Los Angeles, CA.

in the defense of any and all such contests, then each and all of such persons shall not be entitled to any devises, legacies or benefits under this Will or any Codicil hereto, and any and all devises, legacies or bequests provided to be paid to such person shall be paid, distributed and pass as though such person had predeceased me.

NINTH: Should any part, clause, provision or condition of this Will be held to be void, invalid or inoperative, then I direct that such invalidity shall not affect any other clause, provision or condition hereof, but the remainder of this Will shall be effective as though such void, clause, provision or condition had not been contained herein.

TENTH: If any person whosoever shall in any manner whatsoever, directly or indirectly, contest this my Last Will and Testament, or attack, oppose or in any manner seek to impair or invalidate any provision hereof, or shall endeavor to succeed to any part of my estate otherwise than through this my Last Will and Testament, then in each of the above mentioned cases I hereby bequeath to such person the sum of ONE DOLLAR ($1.00) only.

ELEVENTH: I direct that all estate and inheritance taxes payable by reason of my death (without limitation to taxes attributable to property, passing under this Will, or any other limitation) shall be paid out of the residue of my estate, and shall not be charged against or collected from any legatee, devisee or beneficiary hereunder, or any other transferee included in my gross taxable estate.

TWELFTH: I hereby nominate and appoint as Executor of this, my Last Will and Testament, the UNITED CALIFORNIA BANK,

Exhibit 8.1 (*Continued*)

Mistake #63: Using a Codicil Instead of a New Will

A codicil is a supplement, addition, or amendment to a Will that can change, explain, revoke, alter, or qualify any aspect of the Will that it is amending. It must be executed with the same legal formalities as a Will. Although a codicil essentially becomes part of a Will, its terms are considered to override the terms of the original Will unless that codicil is successfully contested.

There are situations when it would make sense to use a codicil rather than simply amend the Will itself to avoid the entire Will being contested rather than just the amendments that are being made. For example, if a wealthy old man decides on his death bed that he wants to give a token bequest to his nurse, it would be advisable to do that by a codicil rather than executing an entirely new Will, which might be more easily contested if it is signed on his deathbed.

However, codicils can also prove to be a nuisance and make the probate of the Will more extenuated and complicated. Thus, Mistake #63 is using a codicil instead of a Will. Inherent in any amendment to a Will is a paper trail of the changes that have been made. That paper trail might give a person legal rights that he would not otherwise have had. For example, if a person has received a bequest under the original Will and that bequest is subsequently revoked by a codicil, that person may gain legal standing to contest the Will and/or the codicil because he or she may be considered as being adversely affected by the later instrument.

Codicils may be a vestige of the typewriter age, when a document could not be instantly edited and printed but had to be entirely retyped. Typing a codicil is much faster than having to retype the entire Will. However, in our computer age of word processing, it is often actually easier and quicker to edit and reprint the existing

---

175

Will than to create a separate document in the form of a codicil. I often point out to our clients that it will be less time-consuming (i.e., expensive) for us to make a minor change to the existing Will, such as changing the name of an executor or guardian, than to create a separate document that will need to reference and tie in with the original document.

When a codicil is duly executed and offered for probate with the original Will, it becomes part of the public record.

It appears that oil billionaire J. Paul Getty, who died in 1976, did not care much about the public record or the paper trail that he left behind. Getty left a 1958 Will and 21 codicils or amendments to that Will. Each new amendment makes clear who or what was in Getty's favor or disfavor at that particular moment. Getty signed the twenty-first and last codicil to his Will in March of 1976, a few months before his death at the age of 83. In that final codicil, Getty turned the control of a large block of Getty Oil Company stock over to the Board of the Getty Museum, which not only avoided substantial estate taxes but endowed the wealthiest art museum that the world has ever known (Exhibit 8.2). That last codicil was a good one for Getty, and lucky for the art-loving public, who have been able to view amazing art collections at the great California museums that bear the Getty name.

Depending upon the circumstances, it may be a mistake to create a codicil to your Will, or even 21 codicils as Jean Paul Getty did, rather than just leaving a single, seamless Last Will and Testament.

I, JEAN PAUL GETTY, of Los Angeles, California, do hereby make, publish and declare this to be a Twenty-first Codicil to my Last Will and Testament dated September 22, 1958, as amended by a Codicil dated June 18, 1960, and a Codicil dated November 4, 1962, a Third Codicil dated December 20, 1962, a Fourth Codicil dated January 15, 1963, a Fifth Codicil dated March 6, 1963, a Sixth Codicil dated September 16, 1965, a Seventh Codicil dated March 11, 1966, an Eighth Codicil dated January 5, 1967, a Ninth Codicil dated November 3, 1967, a Tenth Codicil dated February 24, 1969, an Eleventh Codicil dated March 28, 1969, a Twelfth Codicil dated June 26, 1970, a Thirteenth Codicil dated March 8, 1971, a Fourteenth Codicil dated July 29, 1971, a Fifteenth Codicil dated March 20, 1973, a Sixteenth Codicil dated June 14, 1973, a Seventeenth Codicil dated October 9, 1973, an Eighteenth Codicil dated July 4, 1974, a Nineteenth Codicil dated January 21, 1975, and a Twentieth Codicil dated August 27, 1975.

FIRST: I hereby amend my said Last Will and Testament and Codicils thereto by changing Article NINTH of my said Last Will and Testament as amended by said Codicils to read as follows:

"NINTH: I give, devise and bequeath all of the rest, residue and remainder of my estate, of every kind, character and description, of which I may die seized or possessed and wheresoever situated, including all lapsed devises and bequests (referred to in this my Will as my "residuary estate"), to the Trustees of THE J. PAUL GETTY MUSEUM, to be added to the Endowment Fund of said Museum; but if such devise and bequest shall be deemed by any court of competent

Exhibit 8.2 Copy of the first page and the signature page of the twenty-first codicil to the Will of Jean Paul Getty

Source: Jean Paul Getty, Codicil dated March 11, 1976, proved January 8, 1976, Case Number P 622826, Superior Court of California, County of Los Angeles, Los Angeles, CA.

"TWENTIETH: I hereby direct m   , as soon as practicable after my death, to sell   ht, title and interest in and to the Getty Bui   ed at 3810 Wilshire Boulevard, Los Angeles, Ca   the fair market value of said building at t   uch sale."

FOURTH: Except as herein   d, I hereby ratify and confirm my Last Will and Te t September 22, 1958, as amended by a Codicil dat   e 1960, and a Codicil dated November 4, 1962, a Third   d December 20, 1962, a Fourth Codicil dated January 9 Fifth Codicil dated March 6, 1963, a Sixth Codici d ember 16, 1965, a Seventh Codicil dated March   Eighth Codicil dated January 5, 1967, a Ninth C November 3, 1967, a Tenth Codicil dated February 24 leventh Codicil dated March 28, 1969, a Twelft ted June 26, 1970, a Thirteenth Codicil date 971, a Fourteenth Codicil dated July 29, 1971,   Codicil dated March 20, 1973, a Sixteenth Codicil 4, 1973, a Seventeenth Codicil dated October 9, 19 teenth Codicil dated July 4, 1974, a Nineteenth Codic nuary 21, 1975, and a Twentieth Codicil dated Augu 75.

IN WIT REOF, I have hereunto subscribed and affixed my seal , a Twenty-first Codicil to my said Last Will and Testa his day of , One Thousand Nine Hund venty-six.

The fore nstrument, consisting of nine typewritten pages, includi page on which the undersigned have subscribed their

- 8 -

Exhibit 8.2 (Continued)

178

names as witnesses, was on the day of the date thereof subscribed, sealed, published and declared by JEAN PAUL GETTY, the Testator therein named as and for a Twenty-first Codicil to his Last Will and Testament dated September 22, 1958, as amended by a Codicil dated June 18, 1960, and a Codicil dated November 4, 1962, a Third Codicil dated December 20, 1962, a Fourth Codicil dated January 15, 1963, a Fifth Codicil dated March 6, 1963, a Sixth Codicil dated September 16, 1965, a Seventh Codicil dated March 11 1966, an Eighth Codicil dated January 5, 1967, a Ninth Codicil dated November 3, 1967, a Tenth Codicil dated February 24, 1969, an Eleventh Codicil dated March 28, 1969, a Twelfth Codicil dated June 26, 1970, a Thirteenth Codicil dated March 8, 1971, a Fourteenth Codicil dated July 29, 1971, a Fifteenth Codicil dated March 20, 1973, a Sixteenth Codicil dated June 14, 1973, a Seventeenth Codicil dated October 9, 1973, an Eighteenth Codicil dated July 4, 1974, a Nineteenth Codicil dated January 21, 1975, and a Twentieth Codicil dated August 27, 1975, in the presence of us, the undersigned, and each of us, who, at his request, in his presence and in the presence of each other, thereupon subscribed our names as witnesses thereto this 11ᵗʰ day of MARCH , 1976.

_____
(R.C. GOUGH)   Residing at "LA RHONDA" NELSON CLOSE,
                  HEATH END, FARNHAM, Surrey,
                              ENGLAND.

_____
(M.C. BATES)   Residing at BRACKENHURST, WONHAM WAY,
                  GOMSHALL, SURREY

_____
(R.A.J. TRIM)   Residing at 63 WILLOW WAY
                  FARNHAM   SURREY.

Mistake #64: Impulsively Changing Your Will by Whipping Out a Quick "Down-and-Dirty" Codicil

Despite all the right reasons not to prepare a codicil to your Will, there may be situations where you just do not want to wait for a new Will to be prepared, because you are feeling very annoyed or aggrieved at someone and want to be sure that your wishes are understood in case you get hit by the proverbial bus later today. Despite your strong feelings, it is a mistake to act rashly by having a quick codicil be prepared by your "down-and-dirty" attorney friend.

When Rock Hudson, who died of the Acquired Immune Deficiency Syndrome (AIDS) in 1985, signed a codicil to his Will in 1984 (Exhibit 8.3), it appeared that Rock was not pleased with Tom H. Clark, for reasons that probably only the two of them fully understood. In Hudson's original 1981 Will, Clark was to receive and distribute in accordance with Rock's wishes all of Rock's "automobiles, household furniture and furnishings, clothing, art objects, jewelry, motion picture equipment, collection of motion picture films, cassettes, and all other tangible personal property and personal effects." The codicil bluntly changes that and allows all of Hudson's tangible personal property to pass in accordance with the terms of a trust that Hudson had apparently set up during his lifetime.

We will never know for sure why Rock took Tom Clark out in the codicil to his Will, but because it was done by a codicil instead of by an entirely new Will (thus making Mistake #63), we know that he did it. It may have been done in anger or impulsively; it may not have been the right thing for Rock to do. How could Rock have avoided us knowing about it? Before acting on his impulse, he should have taken many deep breaths and discussed the matter with his most trusted personal advisors. When it comes to estate planning, it is beneficial to take your time, carefully think about your plans, and never act in anger or the heat of the moment. Yes, a codicil that is written on the back of a napkin and properly executed and witnessed could be probated, but it would be best not to try.

FIRST CODICIL
TO LAST WILL AND TESTAMENT DATED AUGUST 18, 1981
OF
ROY H. FITZGERALD (a/k/a ROCK HUDSON)

I, ROY H. FITZGERALD, also known as ROCK HUDSON, a resident of the County of Los Angeles, State of California, do hereby make, publish and declare this to be the First codicil to my Last Will and Testament which bears the date of August 18, 1981.

FIRST: I hereby delete in its entirety Article FOURTH of my said Last Will and Testament. I purposely make no provision for the benefit of TOM H. GLARK.

SECOND: As amended by this codicil, I hereby ratify, confirm and republish my Last Will and Testament dated August 18, 1981.

IN WITNESS WHEREOF, I sign, seal, publish and declare this as a First Codicil to my Last Will and Testament dated August 18, 1981, in the presence of the persons witnessing it, at my request on this ___23___ day of ___August___, 1984.

Exhibit 8.3 Copy of the first codicil to the Will of Rock Hudson
Source: Rock Hudson, Will dated August 18, 1981, proved December 6, 1986, Case Number P 702518, Superior Court of California, County of Los Angeles, Los Angeles, CA.

Mistake #65: Not Contacting the Attorney for the Beneficiary of a Will When Trying to Settle a Dispute with the Attorney for the Executor

When trying to resolve a dispute or to conclude a negotiation in an estate situation, it is always important to identify each of the parties to understand how their interest would be affected by your or your client's claim. Sometimes people make a mistake when trying to settle a dispute by negotiating with the wrong party or by not including all of the relevant parties in the negotiations.

I was having a difficult negotiation in an attempt to settle a Will contest with the attorney for the executor in an estate in which my firm was representing the objectant to the decedent's Will.

The executor of the Will was not the beneficiary of the residuary estate, so he did not have any personal or financial incentive not to want to pay his lawyer substantial legal fees from the estate in order to litigate a Will contest. Such a protracted Will contest would cost an amount far in excess of the amount that would be required to settle the matter. I quickly understood the reason that the matter was not settling, and I then realized that we would get further if we were to contact the attorney for the charity named as the sole beneficiary of the residuary estate. Once that attorney heard from me what was happening in the estate, she contacted the attorney for the estate and expressed her client's strong interest in seeing the matter settled quickly at a reasonable cost. As her client was the one that could object to the handling of the estate administration by the executor, the attorney for the estate was much more inclined to listen to her than to me.

It would have been a tactical mistake for me *not* to contact the attorney on behalf of the beneficiary of the estate. Essentially, it was that contact that led to the settlement payment to our client and the amicable resolution of the Will contest.

When trying to settle a dispute involving an estate, be sure to understand who all of the players are in the course of your negotiations. It may be a mistake to limit your discussions to only the attorney for the executor, as there may be other interested parties who have a greater incentive to want to see the matter resolved promptly and economically.

Mistake #66: Requiring Survivorship by a Certain Number of Days

When your name is Jim Morrison and you are the incendiary lead singer of 1960s break-on-through rock band The Doors, it may not be prudent to leave your entire estate to your girlfriend, as discussed further in Mistake #89. But in the Lizard King's case, it might make sense to require that your wild child girlfriend survive you by "a period of three months following the date of my death . . . " to collect the bequest.[1]

A Will can be drafted to provide that if the intended recipient does not survive the specified period, whether it be three days, three weeks, three months, or more, then the bequest will lapse and the terms of the Will would apply as though the intended recipient predeceased the testator. In Jim Morrison's case, his 20-something girlfriend, then wife Pamela Courson survived him by approximately three years following Morrison's death in a bathtub in Paris in 1971 at the age of 27.

The reason that I do not usually recommend the use of such a specific survivorship clause in the Wills we prepare is because it may delay the probate of the Will and the administration of the estate. When faced with such a survivorship clause, the probate Court may require that the period of time stated in the Will actually elapse before any probate decree is issued and the determination of who the interested parties are is made. It has happened to us when we have attempted to probate a Will that was not prepared by my firm and the probate process was delayed unnecessarily as a result.

Although I cannot unequivocally state that using such a survivorship clause is always a mistake, such a clause can be a nuisance and an impediment to the prompt administration of the estate, and should therefore be used with caution.

184

Mistake #67: Not Including Your Long-Time Secretary or Assistant as a Beneficiary in Your Will

On a practical level, there may be shrewd, savvy reasons to include a bequest to your secretary or assistant in your Will, and it may be a costly, problematic mistake not to do so.

After you are not around to answer all the questions that pertain to your business or office, your family or other beneficiaries of your estate may need to ask somebody those questions. That person may indeed be your secretary or assistant, who continues to be devoted to you and your family's best interests, even after your death. Money talks, nobody walks.

I have often suggested to my clients that they consider making a bequest of an appropriate cash amount to a valued, longtime employee. Sometimes, it is advisable to make that employee aware that he or she is included in your Will, but that the bequest is conditioned upon his or her being in your full- or part-time employment at the time of your death. It may seem a little macabre and calculating, but it works, and it may be a win-win situation for all involved. Of course, you should be sure that that employee is not insulted by the paltry amount of the bequest, or the whole strategy could backfire.

The section of Harry Helmsley's Will reproduced in Exhibit 8.4 shows that Harry left a bequest to his longtime secretary Ceil Fried.

I do not know whether Mrs. Fried felt that the $25,000 bequest to her was appropriate from a man who was worth billions, but what do you think? The conditional bequests to other Helmsley employees, Edward Brady and Barbara Evans, were worth even less than $25,000 because Leona survived, and neither was legally entitled to receive "bupkis" from Harry's estate.

185

ARTICLE FOURTH: GENERAL LEGACIES

(A) I leave to my secretary, CEIL FRIED, if she shall survive me, the sum of TWENTY-FIVE THOUSAND DOLLARS ($25,000).

(B) If my wife does not survive me, I give to each of the individuals named below who survives me and who is employed at my death by me or by any corporation or partnership of which I am then a substantial owner, the sum set forth next to his name:

(1) To EDWARD BRADY, the sum of TWO HUNDRED FIFTY THOUSAND DOLLARS ($250,000).

(2) To BARBARA EVANS, the sum of TWO HUNDRED FIFTY THOUSAND DOLLARS ($250,000).

For purposes of this Section, I shall be deemed to own all property held in any trust of which I was a settlor or of which I am a beneficiary at my death. The determination of my Executor concerning the application of this Section shall be conclusive on all affected persons.

Exhibit 8.4 Excerpt from the Will of Harry Helmsley

Source: Harry Helmsley, Will dated January 25, 1994, proved 1997, New York County Surrogate's Court, New York, New York.

Providing a bequest to a person who has helped you during your lifetime is just the right thing to do, and it's a mistake not to do it. On a personal, self-serving basis, it may be a mistake to omit a key employee from your Will because your survivors might be deprived of the benefit of that person's experience and knowledge, which could be of enormous value to your family during the administration of your estate.

Mistake #68: Entirely Disinheriting Children or Grandchildren Out of Anger or Vindictiveness

I n view of estate tax laws that encourage leaving assets to your surviving spouse to take advantage of the unlimited marital deduction, thereby deferring any estate tax that may be payable until the subsequent death of the surviving spouse, it is customary to minimize or omit gifts to surviving children or grandchildren when there is a surviving spouse. However, when there is no surviving spouse and there are surviving children or grandchildren, it is *unusual* for a person not to leave much, if not all, of his assets to his or her surviving children or grandchildren.

Nevertheless, dysfunction has run, and continues to run rampant in families in America in the twentieth and twenty-first centuries. An increase in estate-related litigation is evidence that there is much latent and blatant hostility between parents and their offspring. Out of anger and vindictiveness, people often fall victim to Mistake #68 and entirely disinherit children or grandchildren from their Will.

As examples of this circumstance, let's review the Wills of actress Joan Crawford, hotel mogul Leona Helmsley, and actor Henry Fonda

The Will of not-so-Dearest mommie Joan Crawford expressly disinherits two of her four adopted children. A thrice-divorced movie star and actress, Joan Crawford Steele died of a heart attack in 1977. At the time of her death, she was the widow of the former chairman of Pepsi-Cola, Inc., and she had four adopted children named Cathy, Cynthia, Christina, and Christopher Crawford. Unfortunately, son Christopher and daughter Christina were apparently not part of the Pepsi generation, and their Mommie expressly cut them out of her Will, as shown in Exhibit 8.5.

The 101 Biggest Estate Planning Mistakes

TENTH: It is my intention to make no provision herein for my son Christopher or my daughter Christina for reasons which are well known to them.

ELEVENTH: I direct that my remains be cremated.

IN WITNESS WHEREOF, I have hereunto set my hand and seal this 28th day of October, 1976.

SIGNED, SEALED, PUBLISHED AND DECLARED
by JOAN CRAWFORD STEELE, the Testatrix,
as and for her Last Will and Testament,

Exhibit 8.5 Excerpt from the Will of Joan Crawford

Source: Joan Crawford, Will dated October 28, 1976, proved June 5, 1979, File Number 2505-1977, Surrogate's Court, New York County, New York, NY.

That may be cold, but the two who were included in the Will weren't treated too warmly either. They each were the beneficiaries of a $77,500 trust fund that terminated when each reached the age of 50. Is it a surprise that the woman who would not tolerate any wire hangers had strict provisions for her supposedly favored children's trusts in her Will?

But in fairness to the legacy of Joan Crawford, we must point out that the bulk of her estate's assets, which were undoubtedly substantial, was to be divided among the following six charities: the Muscular Dystrophy Association of America, the American Cancer Society, the American Heart Association, the Wiltwyck School for Boys, the United Service Organizations (USO) of New York City, and the Motion Picture Country Home and Hospital (with the Motion Picture Home receiving three of the eight residuary shares, and the other charities each receiving one share.) Apparently, Joan felt right at home in motion pictures.

188

If you want another example of celebrities who disinherit their descendants, look no further than the so-called Queen of Mean, Leona Helmsley, who struck again after her death by expressly disinheriting two of her four natural grandchildren. In view of her reputation, and the death of Leona Helmsley in 2007 from "heart failure," according to her publicist and obituary, should it be surprising to us that she expressly disinherited two of her four surviving grandchildren? Their father, and her only child, Jay Panzirer, had died in 1982.

Let us conclude our visit to the homes of well-known people who have chosen to expressly disinherit their children in their Wills with legendary actor Henry Fonda, who expressly disinherited daughter Jane and son Peter from his Will when he went beyond Golden Pond in 1982 at the age of 77. Fonda had been married five times during his lifetime; when he died, he was married to Shirlee Adams Fonda, with three children from previous marriages: Jane Fonda Hayden, Amy Fonda Fishman, and Peter Henry Fonda. The Will provides for a $200,000 bequest for daughter Amy and diplomatically states:

> I am providing primarily for my wife Shirlee and my daughter Amy because they are dependent upon me for their support. I have made no provision in this Will for Jane or Peter, or for their families, solely because in my opinion they are financially independent, and my decision is not in any sense a measure of my deep affection for them.[2]

Whether the smooth talk from father Henry made daughter Jane and son Peter feel any better after being cut out of their father's Will, we will never know. But, hey—at least Henry Fonda had rational reasons for disinheriting his children, as he expressly stated in his Will.

Besides the fact that it is just not a nice thing to do, cutting a child out of your Will could end up costing your estate more as a result of a Will contest or other similar litigation. As discussed in

Mistakes #61 and #62, there often is a benefit to be achieved by providing for some meaningful amount for an heir who is not favored and then including a no contest clause in your Will. Even though it may be distasteful for an unhappy parent to leave anything to a child with whom they are estranged and angry, they may be doing their other children a bigger favor by devising a strategy designed to inhibit or forestall a long and protracted battle among the favored and disfavored children over their parent's estate.

Mistake #69: Failing to Mention the Names of the Heirs You Intend to Disinherit in Your Will

One of comedian Henny Youngman's most popular stories involves the reading of a Will and goes as follows:

> A rich old garment manufacturer died, and his family met in the lawyer's office for the reading of his will. He left $300,000 to his wife, $100,000 to his brothers, and $10,000 each to his sisters. Then the Will read, "to my nephew Irving, who always wanted to be mentioned in my Will: 'Hello, Irving.'"

Although said in jest, the message is a serious one. It is a mistake to neglect mentioning the name of any heir you intend to disinherit in your Will. If a person who has a legal right to inherit from your estate is being intentionally left out of your Will, it is a good idea to mention that person by name so that there could be no suggestion that leaving him or her out was merely an oversight. Doing so helps avoid a Will contest, depending on the particular facts and circumstances involved.

When Jascha Heifetz died at age 86 in 1987, the high-strung virtuoso was generally acclaimed to have been the greatest violinist of the twentieth century, with an elegance and purity of musical phrasing that was without rival. In his two-page Will, handwritten on his personal Beverly Hills, California, stationary, Heifetz states in section 1.a, "I am aware I have 3 children—Joseph, Robert and Jay," but those three children are not mentioned again. Heifetz had been divorced twice and had not remarried at the time of his death. An excerpt from Heifetz's somewhat bizarre handwritten Will is reproduced in Exhibit 8.6.

1520 GILCREST DRIVE
BEVERLY HILLS, CALIFORNIA

Oct. 31, 1980

1.- I revoke all my prior Wills —

1-a- I am aware I have 3 children — Josepha–Robert and Jay.

2.- On my death, I give the following:

a. The Malibu House and $66,000.00 cash to Ann Neblett — if she does not survive me — then to my Estate.

b. To Sherry Kloss my Tononi Violin, and one of my 4 good bows — if she does not survive me — then to my Estate.

c. To Ayke Agus — $15,000.00 in cash — and from my desk: (1) Prism glass (2) Gold Holder (of Scissors and letter opener, with magnifying glass) and (3) Desk clock (she got for me).

d. To the "de Young Museum" — in San Francisco, Calif. my Guarnerius Violin — to be used by playing it on special occasions — by Worthy Performers —

e. The rest of my Estate, to Ann Neblett, Tamara Clagos and Marvin Gross, allowing them to decide where and to whom it should go.

3.— I name as Executrix, Ann Neblett, alternate, Marvin Gross, to serve without Bond —

Jascha Heifetz

FILED DEC 17 1987 19

Exhibit 8.7 Excerpt from the Will of Jascha Heifetz

Source: Jascha Heifetz, Will dated October 31, 1980, proved January 14, 1988, Case Number P 722090, Superior Court of California, County of Los Angeles, Los Angeles, CA.

1520 GILCREST DRIVE
BEVERLY HILLS, CALIFORNIA

P.S. Don't forget Jack Pfeiffer —
the Clagros, Myra Livingston,
Claire Hodgkins, and the like —

Jacob Hen Jed

P.P.S. I direct that my body be cremated —
and the ashes scattered, from a plane,
over the ocean as close as possible to
Malibu Beach (near my House)

Jacob Hen Jed

P722090

ADMITTED TO PROBATE

Date ....
          JAN 1 4 1986
    Attest: Frank S. Zolin, County Clerk/
        Executive Officer of Superior Court
By ....
                            Deputy

193

Needless to say, Heifetz's three children were not pleased by their father's Will, which left them nothing, but which was admitted to probate by the California court. In their minds, their father's Last Will may have been the sourest note that he ever played. However, by mentioning his disinherited children by name, Heifetz helped his estate to avoid a protracted Will contest. Even though Heifetz was an estate-planning do-it-yourselfer, in this regard, he did it right, as it would have been a mistake for him not to mention his three children by name in his Will.

It is noteworthy that many Wills prepared by California-based attorneys begin with a recitation of the names of all of the testator's immediate family members, and that is one good way to help avoid or inhibit a Will contest by disgruntled heirs who may believe that they were inadvertently left out in the cold and out of the Will. Even if you do not want to mention the names of your family at the start of your Will, it is a mistake not to mention the name of the person whom you are intentionally leaving out of your Will who would otherwise have a legal right to a portion of your estate.

Mistake #70: Directing That a Specific Attorney or Other Adviser Be Hired by Your Executor

Many times our clients are so pleased with the quality of the legal work we have provided for them and the reasonableness of our fees that they will tell me that they want to be sure that my firm are the attorneys for their estate after they pass away, and that they want a clause in their Will stating that.

I tell them how flattered I am, and that of course we would do a great job, but I also tell them that such a clause in a Will is not enforceable under the laws of every state. Because the executor of a Will would be liable if the estate were not handled properly, he has the right to hire whomever he wants as his attorney. Despite a client's express direction in his Will that a particular attorney should be hired by his executor, that direction is not legally binding on the executor.

The last surviving voice of the generation of Beat writers, Allen Ginsberg died in his apartment in the East Village of New York City in 1997 at the age of 70. Ginsberg named his long-time secretary, confidante, and friend, Bob Rosenthal, and his literary agent, Andrew Wylie, as the executors of his Will. Always one to recognize the talents of others, Ginsberg requested that his executors "call upon the following persons to assist and advise them in the area in which they are experts: Gordon Ball, Bill Morgan, Raymond Foye, Barry Miles, Ira Lowe, Harvey Silvergate."[3] The Will further provides that "those persons assisting and advising my executors shall be paid a reasonable fee for their services." In his generosity and equanimity, Ginsberg also nominates and appoints "Ira M. Lowe with the law firm of Lowe & Mahon to act as attorney for my estate."

Despite Ginsberg's good intentions, and his attorney's foresight, such an appointment is not legally binding or even effective.

The executors are allowed to select the attorney they want to assist them. Despite Mr. Ginsberg's expressed preference for him, I.M. Lowe did not file the probate papers on behalf of the executors of the Will of Allen Ginsberg.

The one way that a client can assure that his or her attorney will be one of the attorneys, if not the sole attorney, for the estate is to name that attorney as one of the executors. Because an executor has the right to hire whomever he wants as his attorney, if you really want your attorney to handle your estate, it would be a mistake not to name your trustworthy attorney as an executor of your Will.

Mistake # 71: Not Taking Advantage of a Qualified Disclaimer within Nine Months of Death

There is an old adage that states, "Don't look a gift horse in the mouth." Well, the writer of that phrase could never have predicted that the costs of receiving a gift could overshadow the benefits, at least when dealing with the U.S. estate tax laws. Under certain circumstances, the timely renunciation of a gift may be the wisest choice to make.

So why would you want to say "no thanks" to a gift passed on to you? Well, the loved one who made a provision for you may have had his or her Will drafted without basing it upon the current circumstances of the estate's beneficiaries. And due to the way the Will was drafted, you may end up ultimately paying more taxes on that gift than intended by the gift giver.

This is when you may want to take advantage of the qualified disclaimer. By disclaiming a gift or interest in property, the disclaimant will be treated as if he had never received that gift. The property interest will pass (by operation of law) to an alternative beneficiary without being treated as a gift or transfer by the disclaimant, which would reduce his or her taxable estate.

That is why the qualified disclaimer is known by practitioners as one of the most effective postmortem estate planning tools, because it allows a decedent's estate plan to be tweaked retrospectively.

Unfortunately, many lose the opportunity to take advantage of a qualified disclaimer within the strict time frame required. Under Internal Revenue Code Section 2518(b), a qualified disclaimer must be completed and delivered no later than nine months from either the date on which the transfer creating the interest occurred (generally the date of death), or after the disclaimant attains the age of 21.

So, if you are contemplating taking advantage of a qualified disclaimer, remember that "he who hesitates is lost." It is a mistake not to focus carefully on the applicable deadline and the lead time required to be sure to satisfy all of the requirements of the applicable state and federal laws.

Mistake #72: Offering Too Large an Amount at the Outset of Negotiations

It could just be that big law firms with big revenues and big clients look at the world quite differently from smaller law firms with smaller revenues and smaller clients.

I was retained to represent an objectant to a Will who did not have any significant financial resources and had a rather tenuous basis for commencing a Will contest. Because there was nothing left to her in the Will anyway, she had nothing to lose. As her attorney, if I did not get paid for my law firm's time and efforts on her behalf, I did have something to lose.

I was quite pleased to receive the initial generous six-digit settlement offer from the partner at the Big Firm when I knew that my client was willing to accept a settlement in the low five digits. My client told me not to negotiate and risk the offered amount, so we promptly accepted their offer. In that case, it was a mistake for the attorneys for the estate to offer too much at the outset of negotiations, when the matter could have been settled for a proverbial pittance.

Their mistake was to our benefit, as our client was so pleased with our efforts and the result that we achieved for her that she not only paid the entirety of our time charges, but added a "success bonus" as well. Thank you, big white shoe law firm, for making a mistake.

Mistake #73: Arguing with Your Attorney about Legal Fees

I have learned not to take it personally when a client complains about legal fees. I understand that it is the high quality of our legal work that is most important, and the fee for it, although important, is secondary to an excellent work product. I always listen to the client's concerns, and even if the fee is reasonable for the services rendered, we are usually willing to make some adjustment to keep the client happy. However, it is also important to keep your lawyer happy if you are counting on him or her to give your legal matters the best attention. It is a simple truth of economics and human nature that a client who repeatedly complains about the legal fees being charged may have a negative impact on his relationship with his lawyer, which may ultimately be to the detriment of the client.

If you cannot reach a satisfactory agreement about legal fees and you continue to be unhappy about the legal fees that you are being charged, it would be better for everybody for you to find a new lawyer whose legal fees are more to agreeable to you. But remember, it may be a mistake to be pennywise and legal fee foolish.

Mistake #74: Fighting with a Lawyer with "Criminal" Clients

The anonymous voice at the other end of the telephone said, "If you attempt to contest the Will of Mr. Brazzi, my client's clients will first fry you, and then shred you into a million little pieces," and then he hung up.

I had been asked by my secretary to assist a cousin of hers who had been disinherited by his father. I agreed to make a telephone call to the attorney for the estate of Mr. Luca Brazzi to determine whether there would be any willingness to negotiate a quick settlement of the matter. I professionally and politely made my case as to why it would be in everyone's best interests to settle the matter quickly and amicably. The lawyer did not seem too impressed, but did agree to speak with his client. The next day I received the telephone call first mentioned above. Regrettably, and perhaps cowardly, I told my secretary that I did not believe that the matter was "right" for our firm. Without my having to go into any details, she well understood, and that was the end of that.

The foregoing anecdote is much more fiction than fact, but it is loosely based on a situation that did occur in my office. For many reasons, it may be a mistake to fight with an attorney whose clients are involved in criminal activities over a small estate, or even a big one. In any case, I must give credit to the late author Mario Puzo for creating a character named Luca Brazzi in *The Godfather*, and for living author James Frey for empowering me to believe that if fried, I could possibly end up in a million little pieces.

Mistake #75: Having Your Former Mother-in-Law Own a Life Insurance Policy on Your Life

Taking liberties with that famous quotation of Congreve, "Hell hath no fury like *the mother* of a woman scorned."

I will never forget the fear that I saw in the face of a prospective client who told me at our first meeting that his former mother-in-law now owned a large insurance policy on his life. What he was afraid that she would do to him, I cannot know for sure, but he was definitely frightened by the possibilities based on the way she felt about him.

When I asked him to explain how it had happened that his mother-in-law owned a large policy on his life, he told me that originally his wife had owned the policy, but that she was able to transfer its ownership to her mother at the time the divorce was heading toward a conclusion. His former wife did not want anything more to do with him, but her mother believed that it would be a good idea to keep the policy in place, in view of her soon-to-be ex-son-in-law's obesity. She purchased the policy from her daughter and the ownership was transferred to her.

Based on the concerns of my client, he should have insisted in the divorce settlement that the policy be surrendered, either to him or to the insurance company. It was a mistake for his matrimonial lawyer to fail to address the disposition of the life insurance policy in the divorce settlement, which led to the more unsettling mistake of the mother of a woman scorned owning an insurance policy on the life of the scorner.

To avoid finding yourself in the unenviable position of having someone who is angry with you own a policy on your life, consider surrendering the policy so that you can use the cash value that you receive for some other purpose. It is a mistake to allow life insurance policies to be owned by a person who might just wish that you were dead.

Mistake #76: Not Getting the Original Will Back from the Person Replaced as an Executor

An original Last Will and Testament is a powerful document whose whereabouts needs to be carefully monitored. It is a mistake to be careless about where you leave your original Will in case it is lost or stolen. Even leaving it with the attorney who prepared the Will might be a mistake under certain circumstances.

One of my most disappointing moments as an attorney occurred when I was replaced at the eleventh hour of the life of my 95-year-old dying client and lifelong friend, who had named me and her accountant as the co-executors in numerous Wills of hers over many years. Unfortunately, in the final year of her life, her famous strong will was broken, and *in my opinion* she was subjected to undue influence by her three rather pushy daughters. My client had been a well-known philanthropist and art collector, who was admired and loved by many people. Her daughters would not allow me to even see or speak with their mother during the final months of her life after her Will had been changed to excise her accountant and me as her executors and to instead name her daughters, which is exactly what my client had not wanted when she had her strength and wits about her. Some might call it a *shanda* (shame). In Italian, it is *vergogna*, but in any language those three daughters should be ashamed of themselves.

Although the decedent's changed final Will was ultimately admitted to probate by the Court, the daughters did make a mistake by not retrieving all of their mother's original Wills, which I had in my possession and which named me and her accountant as executors. I was able to file with the Court an original Will that named me as an executor, and that gave me "standing" to contest the decedent's Will. I retained expert local counsel, and the matter was quickly settled.

I received a significant payment from the estate, which I promptly transferred to my children. The evil daughters' mistake in not inhibiting me from commencing a Will contest was to my benefit. If I had been their lawyer, they would not have made that mistake.

The best way to avoid this mistake is to keep your eye on the ball, I mean the Will. It is usually best to let your current attorney keep the original and you keep a copy, but if you change attorneys and prepare a new Will with another attorney, it would be a mistake not to get back all of the prior original Wills that may be floating around.

Notes

1. Jim Morrison, Will dated June 17, 1969, proved August 17, 1971, Case Number P 573952, Superior Court of California, County of Los Angeles, Los Angeles, CA.
2. Henry Fonda, Will dated July 9, 1981, proved August 20, 1982, Case Number 675313, Superior Court of California, County of Los Angeles, Los Angeles, CA.
3. Allen Ginsberg, Will dated July 20, 1991, proved December 8, 1997, File Number 4207-1997, Surrogate's Court, County of New York, New York, NY.

CHAPTER 9

Mistakes Involving Funerals, Burials, or Cremation

Because of the absolute certainty of death, it is a mistake not to plan for it. You need to let the necessary and appropriate people know your wishes with regard to your burial, cremation, or other disposition and to provide the necessary paperwork to give them the legal authority to act on your behalf after you are no longer around.

For a celebrity, his or her funeral is often his last hurrah, and there are some who take great interest and control of their funeral and burial and do not want the amount expended on their funerals limited in any way. At the other end of the universe are those stars like Cary Grant and Fred Astaire, who wanted no public funeral whatsoever.

Depending on your particular circumstances, it may, or may not be a mistake to prepay the costs of your own funeral while you are alive. If you do make pre-death arrangements, be sure that the cemetery plot deed or other paperwork is readily accessible by those who will be handling those arrangements for you.

Finally, you should not ask or expect your family or executors to do anything that is against the law with your bodily remains.

You may be horrified to see what Jascha Heifetz wanted done with his cremated ashes, but you may not be surprised to hear that Leona Helmsley wanted her dog Trouble's remains buried with her own.

In the end, it is a mistake not to leave clear instructions as to what you would like done with your body after you are gone. You should name someone whom you believe has the wherewithal and the legal authority to fulfill those instructions for you after your death.

Mistake #77: Not Appointing Someone to Make Burial and Funeral Arrangements

The determination as to who will handle your burial, cremation, and other funeral-related arrangements is quite important, and failing to properly designate the person who will make those personal and time-sensitive decisions can be a big mistake.

One of the many legal disputes involving the estate of Playboy playmate Anna Nicole Smith included who would have the right to determine where her no-longer-hot body was buried. Anna Nicole was survived by her mother, Virgie Arthur, from whom she had reportedly been estranged; her 4-month-old baby, Dannielynn; her boyfriend and personal attorney, Howard K. Stern; and a former lover and the father of Dannielynn, Larry Birkhead. There was a court hearing held in Florida to determine where Anna Nicole would be buried. At that time, it was decided by a Florida judge, over the objections of Anna Nicole's mother, that Anna Nicole would be buried in the Bahamas next to her predeceased son, Daniel. We do not know if the judge just believed that it would be "better in the Bahamas" or simply concluded that Anna Nicole's estranged mother's preference that Anna should be buried in Texas should not be respected.

All of the burial brouhaha could have been avoided if Anna Nicole Smith had taken the steps necessary to avoid Mistake #77— failing to appoint someone to make burial and funeral arrangements for you upon your death. Ms. Smith should have executed a document that stated who would have the right to make burial decisions and what those decisions should be. Every state has some procedure or statutory mechanism for determining who can make cremation or burial decisions, but because Anna Nicole never executed any such document, it was left to a judge to decide. I don't know about you, but I certainly wouldn't want a stranger to determine the fate of my remains.

A copy of the New York statutory form relating to the appointment of an agent to control the disposition of bodily remains is reproduced in Exhibit 9.1. Most states have similar forms and statutes pertaining to cremation, embalming and/or burial arrangements. I recommend that multiple originals of the document of instructions should be properly executed by the client and that one original should be kept by each of the client, the attorney and the designated agent so that decisions can be made promptly at the time of death.

With proper estate tax planning, the one certainty in life is death, with all due respect for the opinion of Ben Franklin. Therefore, each of us needs to contemplate what will happen to our remains after we are dead. It is not a pleasant eventuality to consider, but if you do not take the steps necessary to provide for your final "resting place" and name the right person to take care of that for you, then your body could be the subject of costly and nasty litigation, even if you did not look like Anna Nicole Smith on a good day.

APPOINTMENT OF AGENT
TO CONTROL DISPOSITION OF REMAINS

Pursuant to NY Public Health Law §4201

I, YOUR_NAME, residing at YOUR_ADDRESS,

being of sound mind, willfully and voluntarily make known my desire that, upon my death, the disposition of my remains shall be controlled by AGENT'S_NAME.

With respect to that subject only, I hereby appoint such person as my agent with respect to the disposition of my remains.

Special Directions:

Set forth below are any special directions limiting the power granted to my agent as well as any instructions or wishes desired to be followed in the disposition of my remains:

Indicate below if you have entered into a pre-funded pre-need agreement subject to section four hundred fifty-three (§453) of the General Business Law for funeral merchandise or service in advance of need:

( ) No, I have not entered into a pre-funded pre-need agreement subject to section four hundred fifty-three (§453) of the General Business Law.
( ) Yes, I have entered into a pre-funded pre-need agreement subject to section four hundred fifty-three (§453) of the General Business Law.

_____
(Name of funeral firm with which you entered into a pre-funded pre-need funeral agreement to provide merchandise and/or services)

• • •

Agent:

Name:	AGENT'S_NAME
Address:	AGENT'S_ADDRESS
Telephone:	AGENT'S_PHONE

Successors:

If my agent dies, resigns, or is unable to act, I hereby appoint the following persons (each to act alone and successively, in the order named) to serve as my agent to control the disposition of my remains as authorized by this document:

Exhibit 9.1 New York Appointment of Agent to Control Disposition of Remains form

Source: NY Public Health Law Section 4201.

First Successor:
Name:
Address:
Telephone;

Second Successor:
Name:
Address:
Telephone:

Duration:

This appointment becomes effective upon my death.

Prior appointment revoked:

I hereby revoke any prior appointment of any person to control the disposition of my remains.

Signed this   day of   , 2009.

_____
YOUR_NAME

• • •

Statement by Witness (must be 18 or older):

I declare that the person who executed this document is personally known to me and appears to be of sound mind and acting of his or her free will. He or she signed (or asked another to sign for him or her) this document in my presence. I am not the person appointed as agent by this document.

Witness: _____

Address:_____

Witness: _____

Address:_____

Exhibit 9.1 (*Continued*)

Mistakes Involving Funerals, Burials, or Cremation

Acceptance and Assumption by Agent:

1.   I have no reason to believe there has been a revocation of this appointment to control disposition of remains.
2.   I hereby accept this appointment.

Signed this   day of   , 2009.

_____
AGENT'S_NAME

Acknowledgment:

STATE OF NEW YORK   COUNTY OF NEW YORK   ss:

        On the   day of   , in the year 2009, before me, the under-signed personally appeared YOUR_NAME, personally known to me or proved to me on the basis of satisfactory evidence to be the individual whose name is subscribed to the within instrument and acknowledged to me that she executed the same in her capacity, and that by her signature on the instrument, the individual, or the person upon behalf of which the individual acted, executed the instrument.

_____
Notary Public

Mistake #78: **Spending Too Much on a Funeral or Burial**

Depending on your view of yourself and your place in the cosmos, it may be Mistake #78 to spend too much money on your funeral and burial. On a purely economic level, a funeral with all the bells and whistles can be quite costly, and your family might be better off using that money for something else, as I am not sure that the decedent would ever notice the difference.

Who am I to say that it is a mistake to spend too much on a funeral? That is entirely a personal decision, and some may feel that it is money well spent as it allows the deceased to be buried with dignity. It does not always have to, but sometimes dignity may require spending a significant amount of money. In my personal opinion, the money spent on an expensive funeral or burial could be better spent elsewhere, but since my wife doesn't listen to me about spending now, why would she listen later, especially when I am no longer around to offer her my opinion?

Perhaps the most famous Herbert of the late twentieth century was the comedian and actor popularly known as Jackie, but whose legal name, and the name on his Last Will and Testament, was Herbert John Gleason. Gleason died at the age of 71 in 1987. The first page of the Great One's Will is reproduced in Exhibit 9.2.

As you can see, Jackie's Will includes instructions with regard to his burial and grave site. In stating that this should be done "without regard for any provision of law limiting such expenditures," the Great One obviously believed that there would be many people attending his funeral, and he did not want his personal representatives to scrimp on any of the accommodations.

Unless you are a well-known movie or music star whose legend can be burnished by a fancy funeral, it may be a mistake to

Mistakes Involving Funerals, Burials, or Cremation

87233591

LAST WILL AND TESTAMENT

OF

HERBERT JOHN GLEASON

I, HERBERT JOHN GLEASON, also known as JACKIE GLEASON, a resident of the State of Florida, being of sound and disposing mind and memory, do hereby make, publish and declare this to be my Last Will and Testament, hereby revoking all former wills and codicils heretofore made by me.

I.   I authorize my Personal Representative to spend such sums for funeral expenses, the acquisition of a burial site, the erection of a suitable headstone or monument over my grave and for the perpetual care of my grave as my Personal Representative may think proper, without regard to any provision of law limiting such expenditures.

Exhibit 9.2 Excerpt from Page one of Jackie Gleason's Will
Source: Jackie Gleason, Will dated April 11, 1985, proved July 6, 1987, Index Number 87-443, Circuit Court, Broward County, Fort Lauderdale, FL.

spend too much on your funeral. One way to avoid this is to investigate the costs of the various options, including in-ground burial, above-ground burial, cremation, or the construction of a pyramid as the pharaohs did thousands of years ago, and to discuss your desires with the person who will be handling the funeral and burial arrangements for you after you are gone.

Mistake #79: Providing Overly Detailed Funeral and Burial Instructions in Your Will

Putting overly detailed burial and funeral instructions in your Will is a mistake for two reasons. First, the Will may not be located or accessible at the time that those decisions need to be made. Secondly, depending on how detailed those instructions may be, it may be difficult for your executors or family to effectuate your wishes.

Although Kate Smith helped God Bless America on so many occasions, and continues to do so from the grave during the seventh inning stretch at Yankee Stadium, she also wanted to be very clear as to who she wanted to officiate at her funeral. As we can see from the first page of Smith's 1979 Will, reproduced in Exhibit 9.3, the answer to that question depended on whether her demise took place in Lake Placid, New York, or elsewhere.

It may be a mistake to be too specific in your Will as to who should "officiate" at your funeral, because the named person may not be available at the appointed time. Fortunately, Smith did apparently authorize three named persons to "have complete authority as to my funeral and burial," so that could help to avoid any problem.

On the first page of his 29-page 1962 Will, reproduced as Exhibit 9.4, songwriter Cole Porter directed that he be buried in Peru, Indiana, where he was born, and also directed "that there be no service of any kind for me in New York City." As you can see, Porter also specified which Biblical quotations and prayers that he wanted stated at his funeral.

Because the executors of Porter's Will included an attorney from the prestigious law firm, Paul, Weiss, Rifkind, Wharton & Garrison, that prepared his Will, we expect that Porter's instructions to be buried were followed.

I, KATHRYN E. SMITH, of the County, City and State of New York, being of sound and disposing mind and memory, do hereby make, publish and declare this to be my Last Will and Testament, hereby revoking all Wills and Codicils heretofore made by me.

FIRST

I direct that all my just debts and the expenses of my last illness and funeral be paid as soon after my death as may be convenient.

SECOND

It is my desire to be buried in the Catholic Cemetery of St. Agnes, in the Village of Lake Placid, Essex County, New York.

I direct that my remains be interred in a hermatically sealed bronze casket in a mausoleum, sufficient to contain my remains alone, or natural granite construction. It is my preference that pink or rose granite be used, but the choice of the granite shall be made by my Executors, hereinafter named. The cost of the mausoleum and casket is to be paid out of my estate, and shall be in such amount and without limitation, as shall be determined solely by my Executors to whom I have indicated my wishes during my lifetime.

If my demise shall take place In Lake Placid, New York. It is my desire that Father Albert Salmon of Glenfield, New York, officiate at the mass and interment.

If my demise shall not take place in Lake Placid, it is my desire that His Eminence Terrance Cardinal Cooke of the Archdiocese of New York, officiate at the mass.

By separate memorandum, I have authorized HELENA M. STEENE, SANFORD BECKER and SALVATORE T. GELOSI, to have complete authority as to my funeral and burial.

K.E.S.

Exhibit 9.3 Excerpt from the Will of Kate Smith

Source: Kate Smith, Will dated June 17, 1986, proved July 1, 1986, File Number 3220-1986, Surrogate's Court, County of New York, New York, NY.

I, COLE PORTER, of the City, County and State of New York, do hereby make, publish and declare this as and to be my LAST WILL AND TESTAMENT, hereby revoking all of my prior wills and codicils.

FIRST:

I DIRECT my Executors to arrange for my burial in Peru, Indiana. I FURTHER DIRECT my Executors to arrange for no funeral or memorial service, but only for a private burial service to be conducted by the Pastor of the First Baptist Church of Peru, in the presence of my relatives and dear friends. At such service I request said Pastor to read the following quotation from the Bible:

"I am the resurrection and the life;
he that believeth in me, though he were
dead, yet shall he live; And whosoever
liveth and believeth in me shall never die."

and to follow such quotation with The Lord's Prayer.

I request that the foregoing be substantially the entire burial service, and that neither said Pastor nor anyone else deliver any memorial address whatsoever. I particularly direct that there be no service of any kind for me in New York City.

Exhibit 9.4 Excerpt from the Will of Cole Porter

However, it is not always the case that the decedent's instructions in his Will are respected and followed. A problem could arise if you are too specific in your Will and for some reason your wishes cannot be carried out. Then the person who is handling the arrangements is put in the awkward position of not being able to respect your last wishes, and that may cause some guilt or other uncomfortable feelings.

The best way to avoid this mistake is to keep it simple. The fewer directions and requirements related to your funeral and burial that you leave for your spouse or executor to effectuate, the easier his or her job will be and the less likely that he or she will make a mistake.

Mistake #80: Prepaying for Your Funeral, or Not

Reasonable people may differ on Mistake #80. Depending on your personal circumstances and family situation, it may, or may not, be a mistake to prepay for your funeral expenses.

If you do not want to burden your family with the expense of paying for your funeral, and it is important to you that you make the decisions relating to how your funeral and burial will be handled, and you would like to avoid squabbling among your family, then it may be a good idea for you to prepay a funeral home for the costs of your funeral. That may allow you to lock in a reasonable charge and to avoid the risk of escalating funeral costs in the future.

The problem with this strategy is that you are paying a substantial amount of money well in advance of the date that you hope that it may be required. You have not only lost the use of that money for the rest of your lifetime, but you are also taking a risk that you may move to another place in the future and change your mind as to how, where, and with whom you would like to be buried. You are also taking a risk that the funeral home that you have paid will no longer be in business or will have new management when the day comes for your family to ask for that prepayment credit to be applied.

Funeral directors will probably disagree with me about this, but in most cases, I believe that it would be best not to pay for an expense now that you hope is not required until many years from now. However, there may be certain cases where it would be a mistake *not* to prepay the funeral piper.

Mistake #81: Directing That There Be No Funeral or Memorial Service

Although it is perhaps the final personal choice you have to make, the fact is that funerals are more for the living than the dead.

Perhaps not surprisingly, many of Hollywood's most famous movie stars specifically direct in their Wills that their funerals, if they have one, be kept private and restricted to family members. Although they may have provided that they didn't want anyone to attend their funeral or do anything special in their memory, it would be difficult for their family, friends, and adoring public to accept any such restrictions.

In her Will, movie actress Gloria Swanson stated: "I wish no public funeral or display of any sort. It is my wish that my body be cremated. I direct that my cremation be private and confined to members of my family only." Perhaps Ms. Swanson was concerned that the make-up people would not be able to do her justice after her demise. A copy of Swanson's swan song Will clause is reproduced in Exhibit 9.5.

Even beloved actors Cary Grant and Fred Astaire, who died at age 82 and 88 respectively, did not seem to want much of a fuss after they died. But was it fair to Cary's and Fred's legions of fans that they were not allowed to pay their proper respects to their late idols?

The relevant sections from the Wills of Cary Grant and Fred Astaire are reproduced here as Exhibits 9.6 and 9.7.

Whether you are a celebrity or not, you should not tell your family *not* to have a funeral for you, because your funeral is not for you, it is for them. If you do not allow your family and friends to grieve for you properly, they may end up being angry or annoyed with you for interfering with their need to pay their last respects.

It is a mistake to tell your family that there should be no funeral or memorial service. Depending upon any number of reasons, a

Mistakes Involving Funerals, Burials, or Cremation

LAST WILL AND TESTAMENT

of

GLORIA SWANSON

I, GLORIA SWANSON, residing at 920 Fifth Avenue, New York City, do hereby make, publish and declare this to be my Last Will and Testament, hereby expressly revoking any Wills or Codicils heretofore made by me.

FIRST: I direct that all my just debts and funeral expenses be paid as soon after my decease as conveniently as can be arranged.

I wish no public funeral or display of any sort. It is my wish that my body be cremated. I direct that my cremation be private and confined to members of my family only.

Exhibit 9.5 Excerpt from the Will of Gloria Swanson
Source: Gloria Swanson, Will dated March 1, 1981, proved April 8, 1983, File Number 1899–1983, Surrogate's Court, County of New York, New York, NY.

decedent's wishes may, or may not, be followed by his relatives after he is no longer around. If you are famous or rich, your surviving relatives and friends may just want to bask in your stardom just a little longer, and a big funeral or memorial service is one way to do that. However, because your Will requesting a modest funeral might emerge after the Dixieland Jazz band has already been hired to play, you should be sure that your burial and funeral instructions are known to the people who will be handling those arrangements after your demise. Furthermore, when your time runs out, time is often of the essence.

ARTICLE XIII

It is my intention that no interest be paid on any of the legacies provided for in this Last Will or in any Codicil.

ARTICLE XIV

I desire that my remains be cremated, and that there be no formal services to note my passing.

I subscribe my name to this Will this 26th day of November, 1984, at Beverly Hills, California.

CARY GRANT

ADMITTED TO PROBATE

Date JAN 1 6 1987

FRANK ZOLIN-COUNTY, Clerk

By _____ Deputy

On the date written below, CARY GRANT requested us, the undersigned, to act as witnesses to this instrument, consisting of sixteen (16) pages, including the page signed by us as witnesses, which instrument we understand is his Will. He thereupon signed this Will in our presence, all of us being present at the same time, We now, at his request, in his presence, and in the presence of each other, subscribe our names as witnesses.

Exhibit 9.6 Excerpt from the Will of Cary Grant

Source: Cary Grant, Will dated November 24, 1984, proved January 16, 1987, Case Number FP 21023, Superior Court of California, County of Los Angeles, Los Angeles, CA.

be paid a reasonable compensation and to be indemnified against all
loss, cost or liability in connection with their services. No bond
shall be required of any of said trustees, whether acting alone or
jointly with other trustees.

EIGHTH: I direct that my funeral be private and that
there be no memorial service.

IN WITNESS WHEREOF, I have hereunto set my hand this
16th day of January, 1986, at ___Los Angeles_____,
California.

Fred Astaire
Fred Astaire

The foregoing instrument consisting of five (5) pages,
including the page signed by us as witnesses, was at the date hereof
by FRED ASTAIRE, signed as and declared to be his Last Will, in the
presence of us who, at his request and in his presence, and in the
presence of each other, have subscribed our names as witnesses thereto.
Each of us observed the signing of this Will by FRED ASTAIRE, and by
each of the other subscribing witnesses and knows that each signature
is the true signature of the person whose name was signed.

We are acquainted with FRED ASTAIRE. At this time he is
over the age of 18 years, and to the best of our knowledge he is of
sound mind and is not acting under duress, menace, fraud or misrepresentation or undue influence.

We declare under penalty of perjury that the foregoing
is true and correct.

Executed on __January 16__, 1986, at __Los Angeles_____,
California.

_____ residing at _18337 Calvert St._
                                     Reseda, CA 91335
_____ residing at _509 S. Sierra Bonita Ave_
                                     Los Angeles, Ca 90036
_____ residing at _12073 _____
                                     Granada Hills

ADMITTED TO PROBATE
Date .... AUG 2 1 1987 ....
    Attest: Frank S. Zolin, County Clerk/
            Executive Officer of Superior Court
    By _____ Deputy

- 5 -

Exhibit 9.7 Excerpt from the Will of Fred Astaire

Source: Fred Astaire, Will dated January 16, 1986, proved August 21, 1987, Case Number
P 718475, Superior Court of California, County of Los Angeles, Los Angeles, CA.

Mistake #82: Losing the Deed for Your Cemetery Plot

When it comes to the ownership of a cemetery plot, you must keep in mind that that plot is a small piece of real estate, and the ownership of that real estate is often delineated in the legal document called a *deed*. It can create complications and problems for your family in connection with your burial in your plot if they cannot locate the original deed and present it to the cemetery to prove that you are entitled to be buried there. The cemetery itself may also have records showing who is entitled to be buried where, but it is important that you keep control of your own records and keep the deed to your cemetery plot in a safe but accessible place.

The best way to avoid making this mistake, which can be expensive and aggravating for your grieving family, is to be in contact with the cemetery where you expect that you will be buried. Ask the management of the cemetery what their records show. If the original deed cannot be located, it is possible that an affidavit or other legal document signed by the appropriate person might satisfy the cemetery management. It is a good idea to have those discussions well in advance of the time of need to avoid a potentially big problem for your family.

Of course, one other way to avoid this problem is to provide that your body will be cremated and not buried, but if you do opt for cremation, beware of making Mistake #83 . . .

222

Mistake #83: Directing That Your Bodily Remains or Ashes Be Buried or Scattered in an Illegal Manner

It is increasingly common to hear that the cremated ashes of a person who has died have been scattered or spread in some sea or ocean or other exotic place, pursuant to their directions or at the discretion of their executor. The big problem here is that it may be illegal to scatter human ashes or bury a body in a place that it is not legally sanctioned for such activity.

Oil baron Jean Paul Getty, who died in 1976, directed in his Will that his body be buried on his "ranch property located at 17985 Pacific Coast Highway, Pacific Palisades, California."[2] This is the site of the first Getty Museum, with a magnificent view of the Pacific Ocean. Despite having more money than almost anybody else in the world at the time, none of Getty's fancy lawyers, or anyone else, had obtained the proper permits that would allow Getty to be buried on private property. As a result, Getty's body had to be embalmed and refrigerated at the Forest Lawn Memorial Park cemetery in Glendale, California for almost three years until a variance, or an exception, to the California laws could be obtained to allow for Getty's burial on his private property.

Magazine magnate Malcolm Forbes, who went thataway in 1990, did not have the same problem as Mr. Getty, for the following reason: Forbes directed that his body should be cremated and the ashes spread on an island in Fiji named Lauthala.[3] There was probably not any problem with those directions for the Forbes estate or the Fiji authorities, because Malcolm had owned the entire island. Unless you own your own island, be aware that your remains need to be buried or scattered in accordance with the local laws.

When he died at age 86 in 1987, the handwritten Will of high-strung violinist Jascha Heifetz concluded with the following "P.P.S.":

> P.P.S. I direct that my body be cremated—and the ashes scattered from a plane, over the ocean as close as possible to Malibu Beach (near my House).[4]

True to form, Heifetz did not want to make a big splash, even after his death, and wanted to come to rest near his home on the coast of California. This was probably not exactly kosher under California law, but it would be difficult to monitor. Nonetheless, would you want to be sitting on Zuma Beach and have some Jascha dust sprinkled on you?

Every state has its own strict rules and laws regarding the disposition of human remains or cremated ashes. It is a mistake to disregard those laws, which are in place for good reasons, and ask your relatives or executors to do something that could create legal problems for them.

Mistake #84: Directing That Your Pet's Remains Be Buried with Yours

Sorry, no dogs allowed.

Besides establishing a $12 million trust for her pet dog Trouble (see Mistake #16), Leona Helmsley, who died at the age of 87 in 2007, also expressly stated in her Will:

> I direct that when my dog, Trouble, dies, her remains shall be buried next to my remains in the Helmsley Mausoleum in Woodlawn Cemetery, Bronx, New York, or in such other mausoleum as I may be interred pursuant to this Will.[5]

That may have been what Leona wanted, but that is not what New York law allows. According to the applicable public cemetery rules and regulations, New York has strict laws against the commingling of human and animal remains after death for health reasons. Like most states, New York's cemetery and burial laws expressly forbid the interment of animal remains in a public cemetery for human beings. So not only could Leona not have the troubled remains placed "next to mine," but Trouble would not even be allowed to rent a space in the same mausoleum. But we need not worry about Trouble's problem, because at eight years of age (some would say equivalent to 56 human years), Trouble has a long-term life expectancy, and even though her $12 million was reduced to $2 million, Trouble will not suffer. Perhaps the Leona legal team might even be able to obtain a variance allowing the dog/human commingling. Moreover, who would ever know if Trouble's ashes were to wind up in the same urn as those of her late mistress Leona?

Speaking of mausoleums, Leona did in fact change the locale of hers and Harry's final resting place from the mausoleum that Harry built in da Bronx to a brand-new mausoleum that was constructed by Leona in the Sleepy Hollow Cemetery, located in historic Sleepy Hollow, New York. Apparently, the view in the Bronx was being blocked by a new high-rise mausoleum, and Leona and Harry always wanted a room with a view.

Perhaps thinking that Trouble would be resting with her and Harry, Leona also directed in her unusual and somewhat bizarre Last Will and Testament that the Helmsley mausoleum should be "acid washed or steam cleaned at least once a year." This was in line with the direction in the first paragraph of Leona's Will that "anything bearing the HELMSLEY name must be maintained in 'mint' condition and in the manner that it has been accustomed to, maintaining the outstanding Helmsley reputation."[6] The outstanding what?

But there was a legal loophole available to the executors of Leona's Will: Leona could have had her remains buried in a pet cemetery, as there are no laws against that, as long as the human remains are properly cremated. Not surprisingly, as crazy as Leona may have been for Trouble, she was wild about Harry, and was buried next to his dis- and then re-interred remains in the Helmsley mausoleum with a view. With Leona and Harry finally reunited in that great hotel ballroom in the sky, the only thing that they will not have is Trouble, in paradise.

Mistake #85: **Getting Too Religious in Your Will**

In the 1700s, writer and dictionary-maker Samuel Johnson noted that "To be of no church is dangerous." Although, 300 years later, in many parts of the world, religion is not as central in people's daily lives as it used to be, your Last Will and Testament may be your last chance and opportunity to go on record and express your religious faith.

In the first Article of his Will, the Monarch of Wall Street, John Pierpont Morgan, expressed the following deeply religious sentiments: "I commit my soul into the bands of my Saviour, in full confidence that having redeemed it and washed it in His most precious blood He will present it faultless before the throne of my Heavenly Father . . . "

A copy of Article I and Article II of the great Morgan's 1913 Will is reproduced in Exhibit 9.8.

I, JOHN PIERPONT MORGAN, of the City, County and State of New York, DO HEREBY MAKE, PUBLISH AND DECLARE this my LAST WILL AND TESTAMENT in the manner and form following, that is to say: ————

ARTICLE I. I commit my soul into the hands of my Saviour, in full confidence that having redeemed it and washed it in His most precious blood He will present it faultless before the throne of my Heavenly Father; and I entreat my children to maintain and defend, at all hazard, and at any cost of personal sacrifice, the blessed doctrine of the complete atonement for sin through the blood of Jesus Christ, once offered, and through that alone. ——————

Exhibit 9.8 Excerpt from the Will of J. P. Morgan

Despite his tremendous success and wealth, perhaps Morgan was just hedging his bets and, understanding that "you can't take it with you," knew there are no guarantees in life, or death.

It would not be fair or proper for me to say that being too religious in your Will is a mistake. Alternatively, it might be best for you to write a private, separate *side letter*, which you can easily revise any time that your religious beliefs, or disbeliefs, might change.

Notes

1. Anna Nicole Smith, Will dated July 30, 2001, proved May 14, 2007, Case Number BP 104574, Superior Court of California, County of Los Angeles, Los Angeles, CA.
2. Jean Paul Getty, Codicil dated March 11, 1976, proved June 8, 1976, Case Number P 622826, Superior Court of California, County of Los Angeles, Los Angeles, CA.
3. Malcolm S. Forbes, Will dated July 8, 1988, proved April 3, 1990, Surrogate's Court, Somerset County, Somerville, NJ.
4. Jascha Heifetz, Will dated October 31, 1980, proved January 14, 1988, Case Number P 722090, Superior Court of California, County of Los Angeles, Los Angeles, CA.
5. Leona Helmsley, Will dated July 15, 2005, proved March 21, 2008, File Number 2968-2007, Surrogate's Court, County of New York, New York, NY.
6. Ibid.

CHAPTER 10

One-of-a-Kind Mistakes by Celebrities and Icons

As you can see in so many of the foregoing 85 mistakes, celebrities often make them just like the rest of us. Following are a variety of celebrity mistakes that are somewhat unique to the people who made them, but from which general lessons can be learned nonetheless. From Diana, Princess of Wales to Tricky Dick, and from W.C. Fields to Malcolm Forbes, you be the judge as to whether the estate planning mistakes made by this assorted group of late celebrities should have, or could have, been avoided by them.

Mistake #86: Not Making Charitable Gifts in Your Will When Your Sons Are the Heirs to the British Throne

Whehn Diana, Princess of Wales died in a horrific car crash in Paris at the age of 36 in 1997, she was divorced from Prince Charles, the son of the Queen of England, and was survived by their two teenaged sons, William and Harry.

In her Will, dated June 1, 1993, "DIANA PRINCESS OF WALES of Kensington Palace London" bequeathed her entire estate in equal shares to her two sons, Prince William and Prince Harry, which was to be held in two separate trusts until they attained the age of 25.[1]

At the time of her death, Diana was a wealthy divorcee, thanks primarily to royal largesse in the form of her divorce settlement. As such, she left an estate worth approximately US $35 million. Because Diana was no longer part of the royal family, her estate was taxed by the British government at the standard 40 percent estate tax rate. After the British government got its $14-million share, her sons were left with approximately $11 million each. Ultimately, that may be a drop in the royal bucket for Prince William, who is second in line to the throne, or to his understudy, Prince Harry. However the entire $14 million in estate taxes could have been avoided if the Princess had made substantial charitable bequests in her Will.

Although she was very charitable during her lifetime, Diana did not provide for any charitable gifts in her Will. In view of the fact that each of her sons would be enormously wealthy as heirs to the vast wealth of the British royals, which is not subject to estate taxes, it seems as though it may have been a mistake for Diana to leave out any charitable bequests in her Will.

If you can afford to do so, and your family is properly provided for, it is a mistake not to be charitable in your estate planning. Not only will charitable giving reduce your estate taxes, but it is also the right thing to do and will help people who have not had the same good fortune as you have—and there are many of them.

Mistake #87: Mentioning the Name of a Lawsuit Involving You in Your Own Will

I have read thousands of Wills over many years of practice and legal research. Yet I have found only one Will that mentions the name of a lawsuit and includes a complicated charitable bequest based on the costs of that lawsuit. The name of that lawsuit is Richard Nixon v. United States of America. The first two pages from the Will of former U.S. President Richard M. Nixon, who resigned in the face of an impeachment hearing, are reproduced in Exhibit 10.1.

As you can see, the Will includes a reference to Richard Nixon v. United States of America, and tricky Dick uses a formula to determine how much the charitable bequest will be, based on the legal fees incurred in that lawsuit. I understand that Richard Nixon had been an attorney himself during his checkered career, but why does he need to drag the legal fees into the Will mix?

It seems to me like a big mistake for a former President to be suing the country that he formerly ruled, and also a mistake to mention that lawsuit in your Will and to condition the amount of a charitable bequest on the cost of that lawsuit. Leave it to Richard "Tricky Dick" Nixon to create a one-of-a-kind Will.

Whether you are Richard Nixon, Frank Langella, or anyone else, it is a mistake to mention the name of a lawsuit that involves you as a plaintiff or as a defendant, unless there is a really good reason to do so. Although many people are involved in some kind of litigation over the course of their lifetime, those litigations usually have a life and death of their own, and it is probably not necessary to muddy the estate planning document waters with such litigious references.

LAST WILL AND TESTAMENT

OF

RICHARD M. NIXON

I, RICHARD M. NIXON, residing in the Borough of Park
Ridge, County of Bergen and State of New Jersey, being of sound and
disposing mind and memory, do hereby make, publish and declare this
to be my Last Will and Testament, revoking all prior Wills and
Codicils.

ARTICLE ONE

I give and bequeath to THE RICHARD NIXON LIBRARY AND
BIRTHPLACE (hereinafter sometimes referred to as the "Library") for
its uses, an amount equal to the "adjusted proceeds amount" (as
hereinafter defined); provided, however, that if there are any
outstanding and unpaid amounts on pledges I have made to the
Library, including, specifically, any amounts unpaid on the One
Million Two Hundred Thousand Dollar pledge made in 1993, then the
adjusted proceeds amount under this bequest shall be paid first
directly to the Library to the extent necessary to satisfy such
charitable pledge or pledges, and provided further, that if at the
time of my death or distribution the Library is not an organization
described in Sections 170(c) and 2055(a) of the Internal Revenue
Code of 1986, as amended (the "Code"), which would entitle the
estate to a charitable deduction for Federal Estate Tax purposes,
I give and bequeath such property to THE NIXON BIRTHPLACE FOUNDA-
TION, provided further that if THE NIXON BIRTHPLACE FOUNDATION is
not then an organization described in Sections 170(c) and 2055(a)
of the Code, I give and bequeath such property to such organization
or organizations described in said Sections of the Code in such
shares as my executors shall designate by written and acknowledged

Exhibit 10.1 Excerpt from Richard M. Nixon's Will
Source: Richard Nixon, Will dated February 25, 1994.

233

instrument filed within six months from the date of my death with the clerk of the court in which this Will shall have been admitted to probate.

In the event such property is distributed to an organization other than the **RICHARD NIXON LIBRARY & BIRTHPLACE**, I request such organization to bear in mind my wish that such property ultimately repose in such Library, if and when it qualifies as a charitable organization under Sections 170(c) and 2055(a) of the Code.

The term "adjusted proceeds amount" shall be defined as the excess of

(i) the amount due or paid to me and/or my estate under the judgment entered following the decision of the United States Court of Appeals for the District of Columbia Circuit in the case of <u>Richard Nixon v United States of America</u>, decided on November 17, 1992, and/or any concurrent or subsequent proceedings relating or pertaining thereto, and any related or subsequent case, provided that any such amounts paid during my life shall only be included as adjusted proceeds to the extent such amounts as of the date of my death are held or invested in a segregated and traceable account or accounts over

(ii) the sum of (a) the amount of all attorneys' fees and other costs or expenses, whether previously paid or unpaid, associated with or incurred in connection with such proceedings or any case similar to or relating thereto and all other attorneys' fees from 1974 on, which my estate or I have paid or which are outstanding, excluding, however, any attorneys' fees paid to the firm of which William E. Griffin has been a member, and (b) One Million Four Hundred Fifty Thousand Dollars, the amount equal to my contribution to the Library made in 1992. The amounts under (a) and (b) of this subparagraph (ii) shall be part of my

Exhibit 10.1 (Continued)

Mistake #88: Leaving Your Estate to an Older Person Outright and Not in Trust

The international icon of glamour and sex, Marilyn Monroe, died at the young age of 36 in 1962 from an overdose of sleeping pills at her home in Los Angeles, California. When Monroe signed her Will in 1961, she was already divorced from three husbands, including the great baseball player Joe DiMaggio and playwright Arthur Miller. At the time that she signed her Will, which is excerpted in Exhibit 10.2, Monroe perhaps felt closest to her psychotherapist, Marianne Kris, and her acting teacher, "Method" man Lee Strasberg. Both Kris and Strasberg were much older than Monroe. Despite the age differential, Monroe left each of them a percentage of her residuary estate outright, and not in a trust.

Because Kris and Strasberg each survived Monroe, they, and the beneficiaries of their own estates, continue to benefit from the lucrative Marilyn Monroe estate moneymaking juggernaut. When Kris died in 1980, she left her 25-percent share of the Monroe estate to the London-based Anna Freud Centre for the Psychoanalytic Study and Treatment of Children.[2] When Lee Strasberg died in 1982, he left his 75-percent share of the Monroe legacy to his widow Anna.[3] Lee Strasberg had married Anna in 1968, six years after the death of Marilyn, whom Anna had never even met.

Marilyn Monroe apparently made a mistake in her Last Will and Testament by leaving her estate outright, and not in trust, to two significantly older people. It is quite likely that Marilyn Monroe had no expectation whatsoever that her estate would continue to be so profitable so many years after her death. But if Marilyn had not died when and how she did, she might not have become so much larger than life after her death.

I, MARILYN MONROE, do make, publish and declare this to be my Last Will and Testament.

FIRST: I hereby revoke all former Wills and Codicils by me made.

SECOND: I direct my Executor, hereinafter named, to pay all of my just debts, funeral expenses and testamentary charges as soon after my death as can conveniently be done.

THIRD: I direct that all succession, estate or inheritance taxes which may be levied against my estate and/or against any legacies and/or devises hereinafter set forth shall be paid out of my residuary estate.

FOURTH: (a) I give and bequeath to BERNICE MIRACLE, should she survive me, the sum of $10,000.00.

(b) I give and bequeath to MAY REIS, should she survive me, the sum of $10,000.00.

(c) I give and bequeath to NORMAN and HEDDA ROSTEN, or to the survivor of them, or if they should both pre-decease me, then to their daughter, PATRICIA ROSTEN, the sum of $5,000.00, it being my wish that such sum be used for the education of PATRICIA ROSTEN.

(d) I give and bequeath all of my personal effects and clothing to LEE STRASBERG, or if he should predecease me, then to my Executor hereinafter named, it being my desire that he distribute these, in his sole discretion, among my friends, colleagues and those to whom I am devoted.

FIFTH: I give and bequeath to my Trustee, hereinafter

Exhibit 10.2 The Complete Will of Marilyn Monroe

Source: Marilyn Monroe, Will dated January 14, 1961, proved October 31, 1962, File Number 2781-1962, Surrogate's Court, County of New York, New York, NY.

named, the sum of $100,000.00, in Trust, for the following uses and purposes:

(a) To hold, manage, invest and reinvest the said property and to receive and collect the income therefrom.

(b) To pay the net income therefrom, together with such amounts of principal as shall be necessary to provide $5,000.00 per annum, in equal quarterly installments, for the maintenance and support of my mother, GLADYS BAKER, during her lifetime.

(c) To pay the net income therefrom, together with such amounts of principal as shall be necessary to provide $2,500.00 per annum, in equal quarterly installments, for the maintenance and support of MRS. MICHAEL CHEKHOV during her life-time.

(d) Upon the death of the survivor between my mother, GLADYS BAKER, and MRS. MICHAEL CHEKHOV to pay over the principal remaining in the Trust, together with any accumulated income, to DR. MARIANNE KRIS to be used by her for the furtherance of the work of such psychiatric institutions or groups as she shall elect.

SIXTH: All the rest, residue and remainder of my estate, both real and personal, of whatsoever nature and whereso-ever situate, of which I shall die seized or possessed or to which I shall be in any way entitled, or over which I shall possess any power of appointment by Will at the time of my death, including any lapsed legacies, I give, devise and bequeath as follows:

(a) to MAY REIS the sum of $40,000.00 or 25% of the total remainder of my estate, whichever shall be the lesser.

-2-

237

(b) To DR. MARIANNE KRIS 25% of the balance thereof, to be used by her as set forth in ARTICLE FIFTH (d) of this my Last Will and Testament.

(c) To LEE STRASBERG the entire remaining balance.

SEVENTH: I nominate, constitute and appoint AARON R. FROSCH Executor of this my Last Will and Testament. In the event that he should die or fail to qualify, or resign or for any other reason be unable to act, I nominate, constitute and appoint L. ARNOLD WEISSBERGER in his place and stead.

EIGHTH: I nominate, constitute and appoint AARON R. FROSCH Trustee under this my Last Will and Testament. In the event he should die or fail to qualify, or resign or for any other reason be unable to act, I nominate, constitute and appoint L. ARNOLD WEISSBERGER in his place and stead.

MARILYN MONROE (L.S.)

SIGNED, SEALED, PUBLISHED and DECLARED by MARILYN MONROE, the Testatrix above named, as and for her Last Will and Testament, in our presence and we, at her request and in her presence and in the presence of each other, have hereunto subscribed our names as witnesses this 14 day of January, One Thousand Nine Hundred Sixty-One.

AARON R. FROSCH residing at 10 West 86th St. N.Y.

LOUISE H. WHITE residing at 209 E 56 St N.Y.N.

_____ residing at _____

–3–

Exhibit 10.2 (Continued)

One-of-a-Kind Mistakes by Celebrities and Icons

There was no one or no estate quite like Marilyn Monroe's. However, by leaving her estate to two older people who were unrelated to her, their named beneficiaries have unintentionally become the beneficiaries of the highly lucrative Monroe estate. If your estate will continue to generate substantial income for many years after your death, it may be a mistake to leave your estate outright to older, unrelated people, whose own estate planning will ultimately determine where your largesse and continuing income will go.

Mistake #89: Leaving It All to Your Girlfriend Who Has a Drug Addiction

When Jim Morrison died at the age of 27 in a bathtub in Paris, France on July 3, 1971, he would not have predicted that his legend and the music of his rock-and-roll band The Doors would still be going strong over 40 years and multiple generations later. In his too-short life, Morrison lit a lot of fires and certainly made his mark. He also made a Will, which is somewhat surprising for someone so young and so wild, but Morrison also had a Beverly Hills, California lawyer named Max Fink who may have persuaded Jim that it would be prudent for him to sign his Will.

The one-page Last Will and Testament of James D. Morrison was signed on February 12, 1969 and is reproduced in Exhibit 10.3.

As we see from his Will, Morrison left his entire estate to his then girlfriend, Pamela S. Courson. Unfortunately for Pamela, she died in 1974, a few years after her husband, reportedly from a heroin overdose. Now, we cannot know for sure whether Jim Morrison was aware that his girlfriend may have had a drug problem (or even if she had one), but it would not be a real stretch to make the assumption that Pamela indulged in many of the same types of activities as her Lizard King boyfriend, so if anyone knew it, Jim did.

When Pamela Courson died, she did not have a Will. As a result, her entire estate, including her interest in her famous husband's estate and financial legacy, passed by intestacy to her parents. Pamela's father, Columbus B. Courson, was also appointed as the "Successor Administrator CTA [with the Will annexed] of the estate of James D. Morrison."[4] One has to wonder whether Jim Morrison would have truly wanted his then-girlfriend's father, and not

𝕷𝖆𝖘𝖙 𝖂𝖎𝖑𝖑 𝖆𝖓𝖉 𝕿𝖊𝖘𝖙𝖆𝖒𝖊𝖓𝖙

of

JAMES D. MORRISON

I, JAMES D. MORRISON, being of sound and disposing mind, memory and understanding, and after consideration for all persons, the objects of my bounty, and with full knowledge of the nature and extent of my assets, do hereby make, publish and declare this my Last Will and Testament, as follows:

FIRST: I declare that I am a resident of Los Angeles County, California; that I am unmarried and have no children.

SECOND: I direct the payment of all debts and expenses of last illness.

THIRD: I do hereby devise and bequeath each and every thing of value of which I may die possessed, including real property, personal property and mixed properties to PAMELA S. COURSON of Los Angeles County.

In the event the said PAMELA S. COURSON should predecease me, or fail to survive for a period of three months following the date of my death, then and in such event, the devise and bequest to her shall fail and the same is devised and bequeathed instead to my brother, ANDREW MORRISON of Monterey, California, and to my sister, ANNE R. MORRISON of Coronado Beach, California, to share and share alike; provided, however, further that in the event either of them should predecease me, then and in such event, the devise and bequest shall go to the other.

FOURTH: I do hereby appoint PAMELA S. COURSON and MAX FINK, jointly, Executors, or Executor and Executrix, as the case may be, of my estate, giving to said persons, and each of them, full power of appointment of substitution in their place and stead by their Last Will and Testament, or otherwise.

In the event said PAMELA S. COURSON shall survive me and be living at the time of her appointment, then in such event, bond is hereby waived.

I subscribe my name to this Will this 12 day of February, 1969, at Beverly Hills, California.

JAMES D. MORRISON

Exhibit 10.3 Complete Copy of Jim Morrison's Will

Source: Jim Morrison, Will dated February 12, 1969, proved August 17, 1971, Case Number P573952, Superior Court of California, County of Los Angeles, Los Angeles, CA.

members of his own family, handling his postmortem affairs and presumably cashing the checks from his estate.

It was a mistake for Mr. Morrison's attorney to prepare a Will for his famous client that did not contemplate the possibility, that Jim Morrison's financial legacy would be vast and that his 20th century fox girlfriend might not be around to enjoy it for too long.

The legacy of Jim Morrison is like no other. In retrospect, it was probably a mistake for Jim to leave his entire estate outright to his girlfriend, then wife, Pamela Courson, who lived close to the edge and fell off about three years later. However, the bigger mistake was made by Pamela, and takes us back to Mistake #1: not having a Will and letting state law determine how your property (and your famous late husband's ongoing royalties) will be distributed.

Mistake #90: Making a Bequest with Politically Incorrect or Racist Strings Attached

As the words in a Will leave a record that the deceased person who wrote them can never change, it is important to get it right the last time. In 1943, when W.C. Fields signed his Last Will and Testament, he never had heard the term "politically incorrect," and if he had, he probably would have realized that he could be the embodiment of political incorrectness.

Reproduced in Exhibit 10.4 is the last page of Fields' Will, where he directs the establishment of the "W.C. FIELDS COLLEGE for orphan white boys and girls . . . "[5] No doubt there were many non-white boys and girls who could have benefited from Fields' charitable largesse, but unfortunately, they were not included, and our image of Fields as a person may be diminished as a result of his patent racism.

It is a big mistake, which you can never correct after you die, to make a bequest in your Will with racist or other disparaging language or exclusions based on religion, nationality, sex, or sexual orientation.

(b)$\frac{1}{2}$ Upon the death of my said brother, Walter Dukenfield and my said sister, Adel C. Smith and the said Carlotta Monti (Montejo), I direct that my executors procure the organization of a membership or other approved corporation under the name of W. C. FIELDS COLLEGE for orphan white boys and girls, where no religion of any sort is to be preached. Harmony is the purpose of this thought. It is my desire the college will be built in California in Los Angeles County.

(c)   I wish to disinherit anyone who in any way tries to confuse or break this will or who contributes in any way to break this will.

(d)   I hereby nominate, constitute and appoint Magda Michael to be the executor of this, my last will and testament.

I also wish to bequeath to my friend, Goerge Moran, formerly of Moran and Mack, the sum of One Thousand Dollars.

IN WITNESS WHEREOF, I have hereunto set my hand this 28th day of April 1943.

William C. Fields   X
_____
WILLIAM C. FIELDS
TESTATOR

The foregoing Will consisting of five (5) pages, including this one, was signed and subscribed by the said William C. Fields, the person named therein, at Los Angeles California, on the 28th day of April, 1943, in the presence of us, and each of us at the same time, and was at the time of his so subscribing the same acknowledged and declared by him to us to be his last Will and Testament, and thereupon we, at his request, and in his presence, and in the presence of each other, subscribed our names as witnesses thereto.

Exhibit 10.4 Excerpt from the Will of W.C. Fields

Source: W.C. Fields, Will dated April 28, 1943, proved December 31, 1946, Case Number 264050, Superior Court of California, County of Los Angeles, Los Angeles, CA.

Mistake #91: Not Properly Identifying an Organization That Receives a Bequest

With the proliferation of charities and organizations of all stripes and types throughout America, it is not unusual to have organizations with similar names that are totally unrelated and based in different parts of the country or the world. It is a big problem for an executor if there is any ambiguity or confusion regarding which charitable entity was intended by the testator in his Will.

For example, consider the Cancer Research Institute, located in New York City; the American Institute for Cancer Research, located in Washington, D.C.; and the American Cancer Society, with offices in many cities. These are all different organizations with separate budgets and staff, and it could cause serious problems for the charity if its favorite benefactor does not get its name quite right in his Will. In many ways, it is the drafting attorneys' responsibility to get this right and to be sure that the charitable organization that was intended by the client is the one named in the Will.

If there is not certainty in the Will, the charities may have to agree to share the bequest in some proportion, or the Executor may have to go to court to have a judge or jury determine which of the organizations contesting the bequest was intended by the person writing the Will. Such a court proceeding can be time-consuming and expensive. As such, it is a mistake not to properly identify the organization that is intended to receive a bequest under a Will.

The eccentric and ebullient Malcolm Forbes named 26 different "motorcycle clubs" in his Will, with each to receive a $1,000 bequest for the "Sunday runs [that] provided so much pleasure and fellowship for me and so many other cycling enthusiasts."[6]

As there is a slew of motorcycle clubs with the name "Blue Knights," a problem arose for Forbes' executors and employees when leather-jacketed and sometimes burly representatives of many of the named motorcycle clubs descended upon the Forbes headquarters in Manhattan. The executors of Malcolm's Will could not truly be sure if the bequest checks being released were being given to the right persons who claimed to be officers of "Heavy Metal" from Newark, New Jersey or "Blue Knights" from da Bronx or Brooklyn. Even after he was gone, the man of eclectic tastes and extraordinary vision, Malcolm Forbes kept life interesting for those surviving him through his colorful and unusual Will, and undoubtedly in many other ways.

It is so important to be precise in the identification of your intended beneficiaries in your Will. If there is any ambiguity or confusion, it could end up costing your estate the time and money involved in rectifying that mistake. This is where the attorney preparing the Will needs to be sure that he delineates exactly which organization or other beneficiary is intended by his client.

Mistake #92: Not Providing a Way to Determine That Your Wife Has Regained Her Sanity

When the great American writer F. Scott Fitzgerald was fatally stricken with a heart attack at the age of 44 in 1940 in Hollywood, California, he was survived by his 42-year-old wife, Zelda, and their 19-year-old daughter, Frances Scott Fitzgerald. In his 1937 Will, Fitzgerald states that his wife Zelda is "Non Compos Mentis," which is the legal way of saying that she was nuts.

In his Will, which is reproduced in part in Exhibit 10.5, Fitzgerald provides that the property for Zelda needs to be held in trust for her until such time as she "shall regain her sanity." The problem is that there is no mention in the Will as to how or by whom the determination that Zelda had regained her sanity was to be made. The failure to provide such a mechanism in his Will may have been Fitzgerald's (or his lawyer's) way of keeping Zelda in the asylum and ensuring that their daughter would be the beneficiary of his valuable literary estate.

There was a mistake in F. Scott Fitzgerald's Last Will and Testament. Yes, Zelda, there was an insanity clause, but the problem was that there is no sanity clause. If Zelda were to claim that she had regained her sanity, there is no mechanism delineated in the Will that would allow her to prove her claim.

The lesson that we can learn from the Will of F. Scott Fitzgerald is to be careful when referring to the sanity or competence of a person named in your Will. Not only do you run the risk of libeling that person and subjecting your estate to a lawsuit, but you could also cause the administration of the estate to be complicated by the determination of the mental status of a person named in the Will. These types of "sanity clauses" need to be drafted thoughtfully and carefully, and can often lead to complications.

trust for my wife, Zelda Fitzgerald, who is now Non Compos Mentis...

****

....One-half of said royalties, cash payments, income, or other thing of value derived from the fruits of my pen....

****

ITEM SIX: I give, devise and bequeath unto my wife, Zelda Fitzgerald in the event she shall regain her sanity all of my household and kitchen furniture to be used and controlled by her as she may desire...

ITEM SEVEN: In the event that my wife has not regained her sanity at my death, I give, devise and bequeath unto my said daughter, Frances Scott Fitzgerald, the above designated household and kitchen furniture to be held by her for Zelda Fitzgerald during her lifetime or until she shall regain her sanity....

ITEM EIGHT: I give, devise and bequeath unto my daughter, Frances Scott Fitzgerald, all my family silverware, portraits, pictures, and all special and valuable books, short stories or other writings which I may have written, or all books of value which I may have collected or purchased to be used and controlled by her until my wife Zelda Fitzgerald shall regain her sanity....

****

ITEM TWELVE: I will and direct that at my death should I have books, novels, short stories or other writings of value unpublished, my executors...shall have the right to have same published....

Exhibit 10.5 Excerpt from F. Scott Fitzgerald's Will

Source: F. Scott Fitzgerald, Will dated June 17, 1937, proved January 17, 1941, Case Number 201293, Superior Court of California, County of Los Angeles, Los Angeles, CA.

Mistake #93: Murdering Your Spouse (or Anyone Else)

From a purely estate-planning point of view, Brynn Hartman made a big mistake when she murdered her *Saturday Night Live* comedian husband, Phil Hartman, at their home in Encino, California on May 28, 1998. There is little doubt about the chronology of events surrounding the murder/suicide of Phil/Brynn Hartman. First, 40-year-old Brynn shot her 49-year-old husband in their California home. Within four hours of the murder, she went to a friend's house, confessed, returned to the scene of the crime, and then locked herself in the bathroom and shot and killed herself with the same gun she had used to kill her husband. The coroner's report found a .12 percent blood alcohol level, and also the presence of cocaine and an "anti-depressant" drug called Zoloft in Brynn's blood.[7]

If Brynn had been thinking straight and gotten good legal advice, which she apparently did not, she would have known that under the laws of every state, a murderer cannot inherit from the estate of his or her murder victim. Hartman's 48-page Will, dated March 11, 1996, left his entire estate primarily to his wife Brynn, if she survived him.[8]

Although Brynn did survive her husband Phil, it was only by several hours. Therefore, she would have been barred from inheriting from the estate of her murder victim, not only because she murdered him, but also because under California law an heir must survive by at least 120 hours in order to inherit. Instead, both Brynn's and Phil's estates passed to their two minor children, subject to the terms of the trusts under the Will, until each child reached the age of 35. Ironically, it was Brynn's siblings who were named as the guardians and trustees, so although Brynn the murderer could not benefit from her husband's estate, her family could in their roles as guardians and trustees.

We certainly hope that none of our readers are seriously contemplating murdering his or her spouse. Not only would it be a mistake to do so because it is not the right thing to do, but also because a murderer cannot inherit from the estate of the person that he, or in heartless Brynn Hartman's case, she, has murdered.

Notes

1. Princess Diana, Will dated June 1, 1993.
2. Lee Strasberg, Will dated April 21, 1981, File Number 1982-2472, Surrogate's Court, County of New York, New York, NY.
3. Ibid.
4. Pamela Courson, Died Intestate, Case Number P 603488, Superior Court of California, County of Los Angeles, Los Angeles, CA.
5. W.C. Fields, Will dated April 28, 1943, proved December 31, 1946, Case Number 264050, Superior Court of California, County of Los Angeles, Los Angeles, CA.
6. Malcolm S. Forbes, Will dated July 8, 1988, proved April 3, 1990, Surrogate's Court, Somerset County, Somerville, NJ.
7. Phil Hartman, Will dated March 11, 1996, proved May 29, 1998, Case Number 0511374, Superior Court of California, County of Los Angeles, Los Angeles, CA.
8. Ibid.

CHAPTER 11

Rookie or Boneheaded Mistakes

Having made it this far, you are no longer considered a rookie when it comes to estate planning. In this final chapter, we lowlight some of the dumbest, most boneheaded, and yes, most asinine, mistakes that have been made by clients and their inexperienced attorneys in connection with their estate planning.

Before we delve into these mistakes, it is important to understand the difference between *pro bono* and pro bonehead. Pro bono is Latin for "for the good," and is usually used to describe the rendering of legal services for no charge (i.e., free legal services). *Pro bonehead* is not a Latin term, and is being coined here to describe something that is stupid and dumb. Pro bonehead occurs when a person tries to do a good thing, but ends up shooting himself or herself in the foot instead.

Truth is sometimes stranger than fiction. From the lessons that you have learned from the prior 93 mistakes, I especially hope that you will avoid and evade the following final 8 rookie and boneheaded estate planning mistakes.

Mistake #94: Making a Material Misrepresentation on a Life Insurance Application

It could be a costly and boneheaded mistake to make a material misrepresentation on a life insurance application, because it may give the insurance company the ability to void the contract if the insured dies within the so-called contestability period. The length of that period is established by state law and is often 24 months from the date of the issuance of the life insurance policy.

People often delude themselves into thinking, "If I cover my tracks, I will get away with it." But it is difficult to fool insurance companies, and they can often reap a substantial financial benefit if they are able to legitimately deny coverage on a large policy.

First, insurance companies have professionals who make a career out of making sure that they uncover your tracks. As such, they often have investigative resources. For one, they consult with a database called the Medical Information Bureau (MIB), which provides detailed medical information about every person who has ever applied for life insurance, and they can also contact your local pharmacy to ascertain which medications may have been prescribed in the past.

Second, most insurance policies require that you undergo a full medical examination by one of their approved doctors. They also require that you answer an array of questions and tests on your lifestyle and/or habits. So if you are a smoker or have used drugs, and lie about those habits on the application, your medical test results may reveal the truth.

Even if you lied on an application and the insurance company did not catch it right away, insurance companies have a period of two years after the issuance of the policy to uncover any deception or misrepresentation and cancel the policy. If you should die within the contestability period, and your insurance company can prove that you made a material misrepresentation on the application, the insurance company has the legal right to deny the payment of the death benefit, even if the cause of death was unrelated to the misrepresentation that was made.

Simply put, not being truthful on an insurance application is just not worth it. To ensure that your loved ones are taken care of and are not left with a legal dispute instead of the insurance proceeds that you intended that they would receive, you must not make any material misrepresentations on your life insurance application. It is always a mistake not to be honest, which as the saying goes, is the best (insurance) policy.

Mistake #95: Not Settling a Dispute When the Downside Is Much Greater Than the Upside

Even in the best of families, it is quite common for the terms of Wills and the administration of the estates of deceased family members to elicit strong emotions from the people they affect, or don't affect, as the case may be. After a family member is deceased, sometimes things that have been left unsaid for decades get said, and very often, deep-seated emotions bubble to the surface and can cause destructive and aggressive actions by a family member. These altercations can lead to an even more destructive and aggressive response by another family member.

Having witnessed many family battles between siblings, parents, and children in the context of the estate of a relative who has died, I can say that sometimes it really isn't about the money. Sometimes it is about pride and power in the family dynamic, at exactly the moment when that dynamic has changed. Sometimes it is about an older brother wanting to show that the younger brother who was named as an executor of their mother's Will somehow fraudulently induced the mother to favor him instead of his brother, when in fact the mother knew quite well that the older brother could never handle the responsibilities required of an executor of her Will.

Regardless of the underlying causes of the dispute, remember that sometimes you just need to settle the dispute, especially when the downside, or potential loss or damage to you if you lose, is much greater than the upside (i.e., the benefit or "prize" for winning the dispute) if you win.

In the case of the younger brother mentioned above, the downside was that by reacting negatively, he could tarnish his sterling reputation as a respected and renowned trusts and estates attorney,

---

254

and the possibility that the Court would revoke the letters testamentary that he had been granted. The upside was merely proving to their other siblings that his older brother was wrong. It would be a grave mistake not to settle such a silly dispute with a modest payment of money as promptly as possible. I am pleased to tell you that I did not make this mistake with my own brother in the personal circumstances described above.

Mistake #96: Making Handwritten Changes to a Will after It Has Been Signed and Witnessed

Most people do not understand or realize that making handwritten changes to a Will after it has been signed and witnessed is a mistake that could delay the probate of the Will. It is a particularly common mistake made by people who insist on being "do-it-yourselfers" with their own Wills and other important estate planning documents.

After a Will has been signed and witnessed, a person might decide to increase the bequest made to a favorite nephew or to decrease the amount originally intended for a sibling with whom he or she has recently had a falling out. The client might believe that the quickest way to do that would be to make a handwritten change on his or her Will, and to even initial that change, to be sure that it will be effective.

The problem arises because such a handwritten change, or *interlineation*, is not going to be accepted by a Court because the change was not made in front of the attesting witnesses and without the requisite Will signing formalities. At best, the Court may disregard the intended change and keep the original Will terms as they were; at worst, the Will could be deemed invalid as a result of the subsequent tampering with it.

It is a big mistake to make handwritten changes to your Will after that Will has already been duly executed. This is a good example of the old adage of being "penny wise and pound foolish" by not consulting with an attorney who understands the best way to achieve what it is that you are trying to achieve and to change your Will in a proper fashion. The attorney might suggest that the change be made by creating a codicil amending the Will, or, in this computer age of word processing, by making a new Will that incorporates the changed section or bequest (but before you make that decision, consult Mistake #63).

But beware of a trap for the unwary, even for an experienced attorney who may be unwary. If the handwritten change is made at the same time that the typed Will is being signed, the witnesses must state in the attestation clause that the change on page X was made *before* they signed the Will as attesting witnesses. If they don't state that, there could be a big problem many years later when the Will is being offered for probate and no one can easily prove that the handwritten change was made before the Will was signed by the testator and the witnesses. That would be a simple and dumb way for the best-laid estate plans to go astray.

Mistake #97: Acting as a Witness to a Will in Which You Are Named as a Beneficiary

In the estate planning realm, another example of a pro bonehead mistake is to serve as the witness to a Will in which you are named as a beneficiary. The reason for such a rule is obvious, in that a person with a financial interest in the terms of a Will is not considered an independent and objective witness to the due execution of the Will.

Falling victim to Mistake #97 can result in two negative consequences. For starters, it would probably void the bequest to you under the Will (unless you would inherit by intestacy—if there were no Will under the laws of some states that would allow the bequest to stand). Beside voiding the bequest to that witness, it is also possible that the entire Will itself could be deemed invalid and found to be null, dull, and devoid of legal significance.

It is a big mistake to be a witness to a Will in which you are named as a beneficiary, but it may be an even bigger and more costly mistake for a lawyer to allow you to be a witness to a Will in which you are named as a beneficiary, as that could create the grounds for a legal malpractice lawsuit.

Mistake #98: Removing the Staples from an Original Will

A Last Will and Testament is a special type of document that requires special handling and treatment. One reason it is unusual is because the person who signed it is not around to discuss it after he has died, and the Will then speaks on behalf of that person. On occasion, a Will is the subject of foul play, and some person changes it in some way. The person tampering with the Will might substitute a page. In our age of word processing (what was a typewriter?), it is relatively easy to change pages in a document without leaving a paper trail of the change. The person tampering with the Will might add a substantial bequest to himself, or change the executors or trustees named by the decedent.

To attempt to avoid such a situation, the formalities related to the signing of Wills over the millennia and centuries that Wills have been used have included binding and fastening the Will with a rivet, a brad, and also sealing wax with a ribbon running through the sealed wax. In recent years, most attorneys and law firms have relied on good old staples to fasten a Will. Depending on the size and strength of the staples and the thickness of the Will, a staple may not be easy to remove; if you are able to remove them, it will probably leave extra sets of staple holes on the documents. When a probate court clerk notices that the staples or other fasteners have been removed, bells, whistles, and sirens go off in their head thinking about who might have done it and what they might have done. Usually, the court will require that the tiny little holes in this important document be explained. It is for that occasion that we must prepare an affidavit similar to the one in Exhibit 11.1, which explains how and why this serious breach of the sanctity of a Will has occurred.

Generally, the staple removal may have occurred because of a lazy or careless person who did not want to turn each page of the

SURROGATE'S COURT OF THE STATE OF NEW YORK
COUNTY OF WESTCHESTER

PROBATE PROCEEDING, Will of John Cheatham Deceased.	REMOVAL OF STAPLES AFFIDAVIT File No.

STATE OF NEW YORK	)
	) :
COUNTY OF NEW YORK	)

I, Polly Purebread, being duly sworn, depose and say:

1.   I work at Dewey, Cheatham & Howe P.C., 230 Park Avenue, New York, New York 10169, as an assistant for Jeff T. Cheatham, Esq., the decedent's son.

2.   I make this affidavit to explain the presence of staple holes at the top of the cover page used to assemble the Will of John Cheatham.

3.   I removed the staples from the Will in order to photocopy the Will. I then re-stapled the Will. No pages were added, deleted or substituted during the time the staples were removed from the document.

4.   I was unaware of the problem that removing the staples presents in these circumstances.

_____
Polly Purebread

Sworn to before me this
day of   *   2009.

_____
Notary Public

Exhibit 11.1 Affidavit regarding the removal of staples

Will at the copy machine, as it is much easier to feed a large document through after the staples have been taken out. The longer the Will (and perhaps the greater amount of property passing under it), the more likely a person is to wish to avoid the drudgery of copying one page at a time.

Remember, it is a mistake to remove the staples from an original Will at any time and under any circumstances. As such, the lesson of this estate planning mistake is to copy each page of a Will one at a time, and never, under any circumstances, remove the staples, or other fastener, from an original Will.

Mistake #99: Putting Your Original Will in a Bank Safe Deposit Box That May Be Sealed

Many items are appropriate to put in a safe deposit box located in a bank, but an original Will is not one of them. Very often, after a person dies, the safe deposit box is sealed by the bank until someone has been appointed the executor of the Will. The catch-22 here is that a person cannot be appointed the executor of a Will without producing that Will (or a copy, in unusual cases) to the probate court. What to do? Hire a lawyer.

There is a proceeding that allows a person to petition the court to allow him or her access to the safe deposit box to obtain the original Will that has been locked in it. Unfortunately, it is a costly mistake to leave your original Will in a safe deposit box that only you have access to. It may also be a mistake to leave your original Will in a box that you and someone else have access to. For a variety of reasons, that other person might not like the terms of your Will, and your Will might "disappear" and never be offered for probate.

Whether you like it or not, the best place to leave your original Will is with your attorney for him or her to keep in a safe place and to send you a conformed copy or a photocopy, as we do in our office, for your records. In that way, if the original Will were ever to be lost by your attorney (and we certainly expect and hope not), the copy that you had received could be offered for probate.

Mistake #100: Preparing Only a Videotaped Will Instead of a Written One

Let's *not* go to the videotape. It is a mistake to believe that a videotaped Will is equal in probative value in a court of law to a duly executed written Will. Despite the great technological advances that have been made since Wills were first written, there is no state in the United States that will accept a videotaped version of a Will instead of a duly executed written one. To be deemed valid, a Will must be in writing on paper, or some reasonable facsimile thereof, such as parchment or the back of a napkin.

In certain cases it may *not* be a good idea to prepare a videotape or other film of a person duly executing his or her Will, but it might be a good idea to do so if the videotape were intended to supplement and support the written version of the Will, and not to replace it. Depending on the circumstances, a videotape of the Will signing ceremony might be helpful to prove the testamentary capacity of the person signing—or it could open up a Pandora's box, creating problems in connection with the probate of the Will.

Therefore, it would be a big mistake for your son or daughter, who went to film school instead of law school, to persuade you to leave only a videotaped Will instead of a written one. Such a videotaped Will would not be deemed valid by any court in America and would not be worth the magnetic tape that it is recorded on.

Mistake #101: Owning a Large Amount of Life Insurance in Your Name Individually

We've saved the best (well, maybe not the best) for last—Mistake #101 is owning a large amount of life insurance in your name individually, instead of by an irrevocable life insurance trust or by adult beneficiaries.

Have you considered leaving insurance proceeds to your spouse or children so they can have immediate cash on hand to pay the expenses that will arise in the aftermath of your death? The cash value of a life insurance policy is includible in the gross estate of the owner of that policy. Depending on its size, an estate may be subject to rather steep federal and state estate taxes. Without proper planning, estate taxes can consume nearly half of a family's fortune.

The death benefit of a life insurance policy, also known as its face value, is payable to named beneficiaries. A common scenario is to have the primary beneficiary be the insured's spouse, and the alternate beneficiaries be the insured's children. Sometimes, the insured's spouse would feel more secure if he or she were the actual owner of the policy. If estate tax applies, this scenario could leave the children of the insured with a far smaller windfall than anticipated in the event of a common disaster, for example. If the beneficiary is the insured's estate, then the entire face value can become subject to estate tax!

For precisely these reasons, estate planners advocate the use of irrevocable life insurance trusts. Because the grantor usually has no rights to the trust property or "incidents of ownership" over the life insurance policy, and the trust is irrevocable, the assets in the trust would not be includible in the grantor's gross estate, and the full face value of the policy would not be subject to estate tax.

It is important to bear in mind, in the case of a pre-existing life insurance policy, that the person transferring that policy into the trust must survive for three years following the transfer to achieve the estate tax benefit, because of IRS rules concerning transfers of life insurance policies.

A common estate planning mistake made by attorneys, insurance agents, and laypersons alike is to set up an irrevocable life insurance trust, but then fail to follow through and ensure that the trust is both the *owner and beneficiary* of all relevant life insurance policies. In the case of a preexisting life insurance policy, this would involve ensuring that both the (1) change of ownership and (2) change of beneficiary forms are completed and then properly processed and recorded by the insurance company.

By failing to actually make the irrevocable life insurance trust the new *owner* of the policy, the face value of the policy could be subject to estate taxes. By failing to make the trust the new *beneficiary* of the policy, the dispositive provisions of the trust that determine whom is to receive what and when would fail to take effect, because the trust would not be funded upon the insured's death. The situation could even arise where the trust could become the owner of a life insurance policy whose proceeds will be paid directly to the insured's spouse and/or children, simply because the trust was not made the beneficiary, thereby completely bypassing the terms of the trust agreement itself!

If you have a taxable estate, then the advice about the advantages of having a life insurance policy owned by an irrevocable life insurance trust could save your estate hundreds of thousands, or even millions, of dollars, which would more than cover the cost of this book!

About the Author

Photo by David Seidner

Herbert E. Nass, Esq. is the Managing Partner of Herbert E. Nass & Associates with offices located in New York City, Harrison, New York, and Norwalk, Connecticut. Herb Nass is admitted to practice law in New York, Connecticut, and California. He received his J.D. from the N.Y.U. School of Law in New York, New York and his B.A. from Swarthmore College in Swarthmore, Pennsylvania with a major in Art History; he graduated from the Horace Mann High School in New York. He has been named one of the Top 100 Attorneys in America by Worth Magazine since 2005 and is a frequent contributor to Trusts & Estates Magazine. Mr. Nass is the author of the *Wills of the Rich & Famous* (Warner Books, 1991; Random House, 2000), appears frequently on television and radio, and is often quoted in the press as an expert on Wills, estates, and trusts. In his spare time, Mr. Nass likes to play tennis, collect and analyze copies of historical and celebrity Wills, and spend time with his wife, Jodi, their two children, Stephanie and Teddy, and his many friends.

Index

Index

Index

Index

Index

Index

Index

Index

Index